Rest

7 Types of Rest to Eliminate Burnout, Reduce Stress, and Overcome Anxiety

Allison Hay

Table of Contents

INTRODUCTION 1

CHAPTER 1: DELINEATING THE CAUSES OF BURNOUT AND STRESS 7
Causes of Burnout 7
Symptoms of Burnout 8
STAGES OF EXPERIENCING BURNOUT AND STRESS 10
Practical Strategies to Effectively Manage Burnout and Stress 13

CHAPTER 2: THE IMPORTANCE OF REST 19
Types of Rest You Need to Avoid Burnout and Chronic Stress 20
THE MYRIAD BENEFITS OF REST 24

CHAPTER 3: PHYSICAL REST 29
SIGNS THAT YOU DESPERATELY NEED PHYSICAL REST 32
How to Optimize Your Physical Rest 34

CHAPTER 4: MENTAL REST 41
PRAGMATIC TIPS TO PRACTICE MENTAL REST 45

CHAPTER 5: EMOTIONAL REST 53
POWERFUL TIPS FOR PRACTICING EMOTIONAL REST 56

CHAPTER 6: SOCIAL REST 63
HOW TO EFFECTIVELY BUILD AND MAINTAIN HEALTHY RELATIONSHIPS 65
How to Use Social Media in a Healthy Way 71

CHAPTER 7: SENSORY REST 75
COMMON SIGNS AND SYMPTOMS OF SENSORY OVERLOAD 76
How to Find Rest From Sensory Overload and Stress 78

CHAPTER 8: SPIRITUAL REST 81
TIPS FOR FINDING SPIRITUAL REST 83

CHAPTER 9: CREATIVE REST 89
TIPS FOR ATTAINING CREATIVE REST 90

CONCLUSION 95

ABOUT THE AUTHOR 97

REFERENCES 99

Introduction

A good work-life balance is fundamental to a happy and fulfilling life. However, busy and demanding work schedules can make it hard to create this balance. You may have work responsibilities on top of a family to care for, and you're unwilling to compromise on providing for those who depend on you. It may seem impossible now, but by carefully designing a life that meets your needs, it is certainly possible to sustainably beat stress and burnout. This book will help you understand the seven key types of rest that can help you eliminate burnout, reduce stress, and overcome the anxiety of not being in control of every single aspect of your life.

Are you tired of feeling drained and stressed all the time? Do you want to take control of your life and manage your daily habits to enjoy maximum productivity at work while also getting the rest you need? This journey you are about to embark on will help you deal with your stressors at work and at home by harnessing the power of rest.

Our lives are filled with the hustle and bustle of day-to-day responsibilities that can be draining for many people. Repetitive duties that we have to complete each day and every week can leave us feeling unmotivated and even resentful of our lives. While it's certainly important to work hard and be productive, it's also crucial to find a routine that is rewarding and sustainable. It's easy to fall into a monotonous grind without seeing that our health is slowly deteriorating. It's only when we finally experience chronic stress and massive burnout that we begin to realize how much we have neglected to look after ourselves. You've probably heard of the common saying that goes, "You cannot pour out from an empty cup." When you are working hard at the office and also at home, with dependents relying on you every day, you might feel like all you do is give—and you give without ever getting a chance to recharge properly. This isn't a sustainable way to live. You also need to set aside time for quality rest because this will allow you to function at your best. With enough rest in your daily life, you can fulfill your work-life responsibilities joyfully.

No matter how busy things may seem, there is a lifestyle that you can create which will allow you to look forward to each day and enjoy your life. It's not okay to wake up dreading going to work almost every morning. Knowing how you can rest and recharge in every aspect of your life will help you to unleash the hidden potential you have. This potential to become a better and more present mother, father, friend, manager, or employee may have been blocked by the constant burnout and stress overshadowing your life. With these obstacles in the way, it's hard to access your full capacity to deliver your best work or care. Through learning the art of rest, you will be able to unleash that better version of yourself you have always wanted to be.

With the increasing demand on your efforts at work, at home, and even in your community, it can become difficult to draw the boundaries within which you ought to exert yourself. You may also be getting caught up in a habitual cycle of overworking, and it may even become normalized. When this is happening, it's hard to muster the energy to correct your routine and create a healthier work-life balance. It is only when things start falling apart that eventually, you begin to realize how unhealthy your lifestyle has been. When your body gets sick or you lose the joy you used to feel at work or at home and the stress compounds; that's when the realization dawns on you that change is needed.

It's not a pleasant thing to realize that you are experiencing massive stress and burnout. However, from another perspective, it's also good because that's when your eyes open fully to the severity of your situation. When burnout knocks, that is when you are pushed to do things differently and devise a healthier living plan. If you have been feeling this way recently and your stress levels are just mounting, don't feel discouraged. You have reached a stage where you can finally admit that the way you have been living so far is not sustainable or healthy. Reaching this point of acceptance helps you to be receptive to change and positions you to creatively think of ways to make things better. I mean, look at you now… you are here, taking the time to read this book in hopes that you can improve your current situation. This is something you probably wouldn't have invested your time and effort in if you were still caught up in the vicious, unhealthy loop of overworking yourself without prioritizing your self-care. You deserve to pat yourself on the back and appreciate this step you have already taken. Be proud of yourself and happy that you have started to embark on this journey to create a productive yet more peaceful life for yourself and others.

I know that you are a hard-working person who has been doing so much for yourself and others. I hope you do remember to appreciate and celebrate all your efforts along the way. The fact that you may be experiencing burnout and stress is enough evidence to show you how much of a high achiever you are, and that is certainly something to be proud of. It takes a lot to be someone who can consistently get out of bed every morning and toil throughout the day. It would be much easier for you to accomplish the bare minimum and avoid responsibilities. However, you clearly didn't choose that slothful path, you chose to embrace challenges, and that makes you a winner already. This book is here to help you find better ways to live and work at a high level, because not every strategy is ideal. What you've learned so far is that what brings you success is also often accompanied by stress and anxiety. This book will help you discover ways to be productive and successful in your life without having to also deal with the side effects of stress and burnout. It is possible to juggle all your responsibilities while maintaining a healthy work-life balance. The antidote to all the stress and burnout prevailing in your life at the moment can be found in this simple four-letter word: *rest*. Both men and women require a good amount of rest on many levels to be able to function at their best.

What your body, soul, and mind have been crying out for all along is rest. It is through effectively incorporating different forms of rest into your life that you will finally stop just surviving the day and instead begin to thrive in your life. Think of it this way: A computer that is fully charged performs very well. You can access all its functions and do anything you want with it. However, a computer that's running out of power makes you stressed because you start thinking about all the problems you'll have when it decides to shut down. You won't be able to finish your work on time, and you also won't be able to use all the functions on the computer. At any point, it can switch off, and this means you'll be left without the means to meet those looming deadlines, further intensifying your feelings of anxiety and dread. All this can be prevented by simply charging your computer before you know you'll need to use it. You can even do this while you are working on it. Other times, it's best to just switch it off completely and let it charge. When you're not thinking clearly due to burnout, it's easy to forget how these simple actions and forethought can prevent catastrophe in the future.

We can apply this analogy to how we function as people. Our whole bodies require rest, not just here and there but often. Without regularly recharging ourselves, we reach our limits quicker and can no longer perform at the level we could in the past. However, it is possible to create a lifestyle that allows our emotional, mental, physical, sensory, social, creative, and spiritual batteries to be constantly charged. That is the journey you are about to begin now. You deserve to live a meaningful life without having to be stressed out every day. Just because stress is sometimes normalized in our modern society doesn't mean that it's okay to live like that. There certainly is a better way to manage pressure without having to jeopardize your mental health or compromise your holistic quality of life. If we truly love ourselves, then we can't keep allowing so much strain and stress to perpetuate in our lives. Embracing rest and learning to create a healthy lifestyle should always be a top priority for you.

No one else can advocate for you better than you can. Prioritizing your holistic rest is the essence of true self-compassion and self-respect. Doing this will also help you to have so much more to give to your loved ones, because your cup will be overflowing with energy, both mentally and physically. Even your presence will be felt deeply wherever you go and in whatever you do because your mind will be fully focused on what's before you. That kind of presence will make you stand out to others and attract those who will feed that joy and zest for life.

Having all the rest you need will help you do so much more than you could have ever done when you were running on low power. I can attest to this because I, too, once lived a hectic lifestyle before I finally decided to make a change. I am a mother of two challenging and wonderful teenagers living outside of Seattle. I spent more than two decades climbing the corporate ladder and working in all areas of the human resources field. Trying to keep up with all my family, work, and modern life responsibilities was rather nerve-wracking. Thankfully, I had an incredible outlet, which was writing.

Everything I experienced and the amazing result of how my life started becoming enjoyable and manageable inspired me to write this book after employing the wisdom you are about to read. I hope that, through the practical strategies discussed in this book, all my readers experiencing exhaustion from their overwhelming responsibilities will be equipped to create the work-life balance they have always longed for.

Chapter 1:

Delineating the Causes of Burnout

and Stress

I'm sure you have heard from numerous people who have raised concerns about feeling burned out, or maybe you were the one battling with this condition. Understanding what burnout really is and the symptoms associated with it will help us learn how to better manage this undesirable state of being.

People experience burnout in almost every aspect of their lives. It can happen because of work exhaustion, when you push yourself way beyond what your body and mind can manage. You can also feel burned out in your relationships. This might be you if you tend to be the over-functioning person in your relationships, constantly giving while others just take and take from you. It can also appear within family dynamics if you are the one taking on too many responsibilities without having enough time to look after yourself. Burnout is essentially your body and mind telling you that the way you have been living is not sustainable, and now it's time to put in place better strategies that will allow you to incorporate a good balance of work and rest.

Causes of Burnout

Below are some of the common causes of burnout:

- unrealistic work expectations, such as working long hours most days

- working in a toxic work environment where people are constantly hostile to each other and unsupportive

- long daily commutes to work

- social isolation (This is usually the case for remote jobs where you are often working alone for long hours.)

- lack of career advancement or unrecognized efforts

- having challenging leadership that seldom shows consideration for how others feel

- negative perfectionism and obsessive-compulsive disorder traits

- having a lifestyle that is run by the same routine every single day

- insistent feeling that you keep losing control of your life

- absence of rewards or any form of extrinsic motivation

- lack of intrinsic motivation

- doing things that don't align with what you are truly passionate about

Symptoms of Burnout

To better identify if what you have been feeling is really burnout or not, these are some of the common symptoms associated with the condition:

- feeling restless and having difficulty maintaining a consistent sleep pattern

- chronic stress and anxiety

- feeling detached and disconnected from many things; not having the strength to keep up with people or day-to-day responsibilities

- disengaging yourself from many roles and preferring to be left alone

- dreading work and feeling too drained to do anything

- frequent illnesses popping up, such as headaches, migraines, fever, and even chest pains

- having low energy

- lower tolerance for drama and any behaviors that make you feel drained

- lacking motivation and thus procrastinating on many things

- feeling hopeless and helpless at times; having difficulty seeing yourself ever being able to get things done (You may have stopped taking on challenges and new opportunities.)

- being behind in your work and having to constantly play catch-up

- compromising your quality of life and settling for unhealthy fast food because of the convenience it provides; no energy to keep up a healthy lifestyle (You might have stopped exercising and may even struggle to keep the house clean and in order.)

- if you are a parent, having difficulty being there for your children as much as before; easily showing signs of withdrawal and frustration

Burnout is indeed an unpleasant condition to be stuck in. What's even worse is that it doesn't easily go away. This means that the longer it lasts, the harder it will be to manage the negative effects of it. Work begins to pile up even more, making it harder for you to have the courage to move in a different direction. If things continue to remain the same, a mental breakdown will become a possibility soon, not to mention strained relationships and poor health. Without putting in place appropriate strategies to turn things around and build a system that supports efficiency and self-regulation, burnout can continue to be a recurring concern in your life. Now, we certainly don't want that to be your reality anymore, so let's turn over a new leaf by exploring the different ways you can mitigate the effects of burnout.

Stages of Experiencing Burnout and Stress

To establish a good understanding of the best steps to take when dealing with burnout, first, let's go over the different stages of burnout. Each stage requires a corresponding action to manage it.

The World Health Organization proclaimed in 2019 that burnout is a syndrome mainly stemming from being occupied by work or any demanding responsibility. It is essentially experiencing prolonged fatigue which ends up deteriorating your mental, emotional, physical, and holistic well-being (Integris Health, 2021).

Before burnout starts showing its full-blown signs, here are the stages that people typically go through:

1. **Occupational honeymoon phase:** This is the most exciting stage of any role when you first take it on. Just as the honeymoon phase for romantic partners is usually the most thrilling and satisfying stage, this is also when you have so much energy to get things done. It's like how people typically conduct themselves when they receive a new job offer they have been desperately waiting for, or when they become first-time parents after waiting for children for a long time. This stage is filled with so much enthusiasm and high levels of productivity. This is when your creative energy will be flowing seamlessly, and your work just feels great.

2. **Beginning of the stress phase:** This is when the honeymoon energy you used to feel starts to die down. This might be due to physical or mental strain caused by taking on workloads for prolonged periods that your body and mind weren't ready to manage. This onset of stress first begins intermittently before

becoming a constant feeling you have throughout most of your days. At this stage, you start to see signs of a loss of focus and difficulty doing what you used to do with ease. You might start taking longer to meet your responsibilities and even feel the need to delay many of your duties to another time. Due to the physical fatigue you start to experience, you may end up having a hard time keeping up with your social demands and getting enough sleep.

3. **Perpetual stress stage:** During this phase, your stress levels start to take a huge toll on you. The stress is no longer intermittent, and each hour of your life feels very stressful, making it extra hard for you to enjoy what you are doing or remain fully engaged. The quality of your work or relationships begins to deteriorate, as this is when you do things in survival mode instead of intentionally maintaining healthy relationships and a good work ethic. Your work starts to fall below standard, and almost everything you have to do begins to feel draining to you. When people are stressed, they tend to lash out at others often and experience mood swings, which create an atmosphere that's filled with strife and negative energy. Emotional regulation becomes very difficult and, as a result, you may start making a lot of mistakes. You start to feel like everything is out of your control, thus further reinforcing the stress in your life. Procrastination and failure to deliver your work on time become the norm during this phase.

4. **Full-blown burnout stage:** During this phase, your stress levels will have reached their pinnacle, and cortisol hormones become frequent visitors in your bloodstream. At work, your performance level becomes noticeably concerning. At home, family and friends also begin to feel worried about the way you have been acting lately, as they start to notice problematic behavioral changes in you. At this stage, it becomes almost impossible for you to function normally at all. You might start

to feel strong urges to nap most of the time, and the moment you think of getting work done, a feeling of dread and frustration rushes through you, leaving you even more demotivated to get things done. At this point, your energy levels will be consistently low for long periods of time. Doing any physical activities may become challenging and, as a result, you become weaker and weaker. For instance, exercising is something that usually makes you feel refreshed and improves your fitness. The energy you get from working out makes you more capable of getting your work done quicker and with better quality. That means, if exercise is no longer part of your regular routine, your body will be deprived of the energy it needs to support your productivity. Since it becomes challenging for you to complete your work on time, the stress that comes with worrying about all the incomplete things waiting for you starts to consume you and dominate your thoughts. Before long, your mind is constantly plagued with worries, and you get stuck in a cycle of mental overdrive through constantly worrying about your life. This is very challenging because it feels like you're not making any actual progress, and the actions you want to take are only happening in your mind. It is at this stage that you might visibly notice signs of stress and fatigue, such as looking pale, having bags under your eyes, getting sick more often, and battling to get restful sleep.

5. **Habitual burnout:** During this final stage, burnout becomes a regular part of your life instead of a once-off experience. This stage only sets in if burnout is not managed effectively in either one of the preceding stages. For someone experiencing habitual burnout, they tend to experience chronic fatigue and an inability to cope with day-to-day responsibilities. If this persists, you might end up struggling to pay bills, miss many opportunities, and become caught in a constant negative cycle of minimal productivity in almost every aspect of your life. Even though this stage sounds very dire and rather hopeless, the good news is that you can still get your life back on track, as long as you commit

to putting in the effort needed to make permanent changes and move in the right direction. Through consistent effort, careful planning, and discipline, it's possible to interrupt this pattern and finally attain a good balance in your lifestyle.

In the following section, we will unpack the different ways you can effectively mitigate and manage the effects of burnout and stress. Ready for solutions? Let's dive right in!

Practical Strategies to Effectively Manage Burnout and Stress

Okay, let's be honest: It's hard to finally admit that you are experiencing burnout, especially if you are used to being a high performer and are constantly praised by others. You might feel very ashamed of yourself as you struggle to accept that you are currently going through a difficult season in your life and need help. As unpleasant as it is to go through stress and burnout, on the flip side, it can also be a blessing in disguise, especially if it helps you to better your lifestyle and improve the way you take care of yourself. Problems have a way of showing us opportunities and strengths we have that we might never have harnessed before when everything felt calm and okay. No matter how bad your burnout might be, it's very encouraging to know that bouncing back is possible. You'll not only bounce back but also create a better lifestyle that will complement your goals.

Here are a few practical strategies to get you started with resolving the problem of stress and burnout:

- **Acceptance:** The first thing to do in overcoming the effects of burnout and stress is to accept the fact that this is really happening to you. Acceptance will help you prepare to take actionable steps that will resolve the situation. On the other hand, persistent denial only perpetuates the burnout cycle and keeps you stuck in the same reality. It's important to accept the situation yourself and consider sharing your difficulties with others, especially the people who may have been affected by your behavioral changes caused by feeling stressed and burned out. This includes your manager and co-workers as well as family and friends. If you are a parent, the people who might have faced the most challenges due to you feeling that way would probably include your significant other and children. Accepting means also being accountable for your actions and apologizing to anyone you might have hurt or disappointed in the process. This allows others to have empathy for you and creates room for healing and restoration of relationships that may have been strained in the process. When you take this pivotal step, a lot of relational stress is taken off your shoulders because instead of living with people who are mad at you at home or at work, you will be surrounded by people who understand where you are coming from and who are willing to help.

- **Communicate with relevant people about it:** Accepting your dilemma and communicating about it will help you get to a position to receive the help and support you need on your road to recovery. However, it's important to note that the way you communicate with others about the situation is very important. It's better to be positive and not shift any blame onto anyone for what you were experiencing, as this might only jeopardize your relationships and make things harder for you. Instead, consider using a more thoughtful approach by taking responsibility for how things went off course and respectfully suggesting ways you think others could help to ensure that it doesn't happen again. Complaining and grumbling only make people see you as incapable of owning up to your mistakes, and this behavior may also keep you from seeing how you could have taken control of the situation. Be open to suggestions for improvement from others and also keep a journal of the ideas that come to your mind about how you can create a better routine for yourself.

- **Take some time for rest, and use that time to think about the situation and devise a better approach to your work and**

life: If you have reached the point of habitual burnout, chances are that the first thing you need before jumping into a new schedule is a break. Going on a short vacation to reflect on how you could have managed your time better may be helpful to destress and get yourself ready for a new start. Make time for adequate sleep.

Sometimes burnout is caused by mental and emotional exhaustion, in which case it would be best to take some time to offload what's in your heart by writing in a journal. Another type of writing that can help you gain perspective is a gratitude journal. By recounting all the things you are grateful for, it helps lower your cortisol levels and induce feel-good hormones, which will be important for changing your emotional state of being to a positive one.

- **Create healthier boundaries and be courageous enough to maintain them:** One of the major reasons why people experience massive burnout is their need to constantly please others and gain validation. This is seen when someone takes on huge workloads beyond what they are able to bear, leading to burnout and stress. It's important to learn to say no whenever you see that you won't have the time or don't have the ability to undertake certain roles. In relationships, it's also important to express your needs and ensure that you are not the only one putting in work while the other person is just constantly taking from you. Healthy relationships should always be a two-way street, where both people are mutually putting in the effort to make things run smoothly.

- **Be as proactive as possible with most of your duties whenever time allows:** Sometimes you might notice that there are many things you can do in advance to help you create free time and relax or get on with other things. However, we don't always take advantage of such opportunities. For instance, during the times when you are struggling to sleep, instead of staring at the ceiling for hours doing nothing, you can use that time to finish something you were working on that you can complete from home. Learning to recognize opportunities for increasing your productivity as early as possible helps you to manage your time and work more effectively. Practice avoiding procrastination as much as possible. Starting your day early helps to ensure that before it's midday, you are already ahead of your game and have completed most of what you needed to do. Just knowing that you are already through with your duties earlier in the day gives you a sense of control over your life, not to mention satisfaction, which in turn continues to reinforce that positive way of life.

- **Exercise and eat healthy every day:** Exercising and eating nutritious meals helps to boost your immune system and increase your energy levels. Sometimes people shy away from cooking nutritious meals because they think it's going to take too much of their time to cook. If this is your concern, you might consider preparing bulk meals at once that can last you several days. This way, you can just refrigerate and microwave when you need to eat. When it comes to exercising, it doesn't have to be the tedious kinds of workouts that take a long time. Devoting just 10 minutes of your time each day to take a run or do any aerobic exercise of your choice that increases your heart rate helps you maintain your fitness levels and keeps you energized for the day's work. To plan nutritious meals, try to ensure that your meals are packed with lots of whole, natural, nutrient-dense foods that fuel your body and keep you healthy. Avoid sugary, processed, and packaged foods and sodas that provide little nutritional value and empty calories. All foods with starch normally convert to sugars in your body, which can increase blood sugar levels. Cutting down on your cholesterol intake also helps to maintain a healthy body. The more you eat well, the less your body will be prone to getting sick or becoming fatigued easily. It may also be a good practice to take supplements for your diet, such as iron, though you should speak with a healthcare professional before adding these to your diet. It can be a good practice to take a high-quality multivitamin to boost your energy levels and help balance out other nutrients you may have missed out on in your meal plans.

- **Prioritize self-care:** Self-care entails many things in this context, from getting enough physical rest and staying hydrated to looking after your mental health. Taking time to process how you feel and ensuring that your needs are being met is part of self-care. Our lives can't just be all work and no play. As humans, we have different needs that are important, and all deserve to be met. This includes your need to connect with others and have a sense of belonging, meaning that your life needs to include room for you to just ease up and experience the joy of other people's company. We also need to create a life that supports our self-actualization and esteem needs, meaning that we have to make room to grow and achieve our fullest potential. Doing the same thing over and over again without the prospect of growth leads to demotivation and feelings of stress and burnout. Prioritize your self-care time mindfully and ensure that you and others respect it. Once you finish completing your daily goals, always do something you enjoy to celebrate and acknowledge your efforts. This, too, is an integral part of self-care.

- **Practice delegating relevant duties:** Being able to delegate is a skill that only grows through practice. Many people avoid delegating duties to others and end up taking on more responsibilities than they should because they feel bad asking others to do their part. We often think that by asking others to do their part, they will end up disliking us or giving us a hard time. The irony of this is that when you sideline your well-being and put others first without considering yourself, it often causes others to lose respect for you. It also makes you an easy target for constant manipulation and being taken advantage of. This dynamic ends up perpetuating the burnout cycle instead of ending it. However, the more you delegate, the easier it will be for you to manage your workload and complete what you need to do on time.

- **Breathing techniques:** When you are feeling burned out and stressed, chances are you might regularly experience difficulties with staying calm and constantly feel hypersensitive and stressed. Breathing exercises, such as taking deep breaths and mindfully meditating, help you to calm your nerves and gain composure. This can be done at any time of the day and anywhere you are. Just find a stable place to sit or stand and then inhale deeply for at least five to eight seconds, then breathe out slowly. This gives your body the oxygen supply it desperately needs in times when you are not feeling at ease. Having a massage here and there also helps to release tension from your muscles and relax your body and mind.

As you can see, all of these things are within your reach to apply in your life, no matter your circumstances. What other strategies can you think of? Write those ideas down, too, and create a game plan that is best suited to your lifestyle and personality type. To help us understand more about one of the most important strategies that can help you to effectively manage burnout and stress, let's next explore the importance of rest.

Chapter 2:

The Importance of Rest

Subjects such as healthy eating, exercising, getting ahead at work, and dressing with style tend to be hot topics promoted by the mainstream media. However, another extremely integral topic is commonly underrated. What often gets left out of the conversation is *the importance of rest*. Many people work hard to establish themselves in a routine of work, service, and caring for a family but without the right focus and balance. This is what leads them to lose their joy, even if they felt invigorated at the start, like in the honeymoon phase we discussed in the last chapter. As human beings, our bodies are designed to thrive as long as we give them what they need, and that includes adequate rest. We need rest, not only in the physical sense but also mentally, emotionally, and even spiritually; areas that tend to be put on the back burner in favor of "taking care of business." Think about it: Do you remember a time when you got lots and lots of sleep but still felt drained and exhausted when you got up for the day? This is a clear indication that sleeping for eight hours on its own is not enough to satisfy your rest needs. Your whole being needs recharging in order to regain your energy and function at your best, no matter what the task. There is more to the equation. Your body needs rest in the other areas of your life, including the mental, emotional, social, spiritual, sensory, and even creative realms. All of these together define who you are as a human being, and you can begin to live a well-balanced, healthy lifestyle once you learn to incorporate holistic self-care on a regular basis. This way, you are putting up strong safeguards against falling into the rut of burnout and chronic stress.

In order for us to gain a thorough understanding of what all these types of rest entail, let's have a look at each one of them. You will be surprised at how easy it can be for you to turn things around in every area of your everyday life by simply prioritizing rest in all its essential forms. Let's dive right into it!

Types of Rest You Need to Avoid Burnout and Chronic Stress

1. **Physical Rest:** This is the type of rest we all think of first, and hopefully, it's already part of your routine. Physical rest is when you allow your body to take a break from being in active mode through sleep. For your body to function at its best, getting 7–9 hours of sleep is ideal. Aside from the physical act of sleeping, you can also physically rest by relaxing on your bed or couch and disengaging for a time from any activities that require you to pump out energy. People who routinely take breaks during the day and allow their bodies to briefly disengage from work, even if it's just for an hour, tend to focus better for the rest of the day, as that rest allows their bodies to recoup. Physical rest also entails doing physical activities that promote fitness and relaxation for your body. These activities include things like massage therapy, yoga, Tai Chi, and stretching exercises, among many other relaxation techniques.

2. **Emotional Rest:** We live in a time when you can easily lose yourself and disregard your emotions by getting trapped in the people-pleasing demands of the modern world. This tends to take a huge emotional toll on many people in any circumstance. Emotional rest is activated when you are able to freely express how you feel, can resolve conflicts, and no longer suppress difficult emotions. Without emotional rest, it's difficult to feel alive and happy in your interpersonal relationships. In fact, your human interactions can start to feel suffocating if those relationships don't make room for you to be your authentic self. Sometimes people are made fun of or are considered too sensitive whenever they try to express their emotions. This makes it hard for them to feel safe opening up to others, which ultimately leads to emotional exhaustion. The consequences of inadequate emotional rest include getting sick more easily and becoming more prone to disorders like depression, anxiety, and

panic attacks. It also makes people feel like they need to retreat from others and even the relationships that could help support them in recovery. Chronic stress without emotional rest can cloud a person's judgment when it comes to seeing solutions.

3. **Mental Rest:** When we go about our everyday work, it's not just our bodies taking on the heat and burden of that work—our minds can work overtime, too. A lack of mental rest means you are constantly switched on and investing your mental energy into getting things done. People who work physically demanding jobs sometimes fail to understand how tiring a mentally demanding job can be. When we think of someone sitting in a chair all day doing creative or technical work on a computer, we might assume that this person is not expending nearly as much energy as, say, someone working a construction site for the same amount of time. But anyone who works a mentally challenging job will tell you that mental exhaustion is just as real and debilitating as physical exhaustion. Our brains aren't designed to be in overdrive constantly, just like our bodies aren't designed to run back-to-back marathons for days on end. It's important to acknowledge that it takes a lot of mental energy to get things done. People with jobs like programming, accounting, writing, and many other mentally demanding jobs struggle desperately when they are deprived of mental rest. It's important to give your mind some time to switch off so that your concentration capacity can be refreshed. Taking a real mental break means disengaging entirely from your job or kids or whatever it is that's wearing you down. The details are completely up to you and what you personally find mentally relaxing. Lots of people like to watch a favorite TV show or engage in some other fun activity. Doing this releases a spike in dopamine, which is called a "feel-good" hormone for a reason. Even just watching comedy skits or funny videos online that don't require you to think much will help your mind to take a break and move you away from that edge of burnout and stress.

4. **Social Rest:** Our social lives consist of the relationships we maintain with our family, friends, coworkers, and anyone else we interact with on a regular basis, even virtually. A healthy relationship is rejuvenating, but some can become toxic and draining. It's important to take some time to consider which category your relationships are in. Those that are draining your energy or filling you with toxic emotions are the relationships you need to break off, difficult as it may be. If there is someone in your life who is fueling drama and stress, it would be a good practice to limit your interactions with that person, especially if they are unreasonable and unwilling to change. Social rest also entails being able to detach yourself from societal expectations and stand up for what you believe in. Remember the people-pleasing trap I mentioned at the beginning of this chapter? Living a life where you are constantly trying to meet other people's expectations only leads to social exhaustion. There are people in your life who make you feel refreshed and who bring out the best in you. These are the people you ought to spend your time with in order for you to be socially rested and rejuvenated.

5. **Spiritual Rest:** Being a human being means that you have a body, soul, and spirit. Each of these components of who you are requires nourishment and rest. Your spirit feeds on spiritual food, which in this case refers to the religious beliefs you adhere to. It also includes any teachings you listen to that help you to keep growing and deal with life issues through the wisdom those teachings provide. If our lives just revolve around tending to our bodies and we forget that we have our inner selves that need looking after, we start losing our zest for life. This makes it easy to miss out on the knowledge, inner strength, and wisdom we need to overcome all of life's challenges we face. Spiritual rest also entails being part of a community that supports you spiritually. This support works like an anchor in your life, as indeed, raising a person to be a strong human being inside and out takes a village! Give yourself the opportunity to open up and

discover your purpose so you can finally start living your life with less stress and existential angst.

6. **Sensory Rest:** Technology has swept over our lives like a storm, and everywhere we go, there is always some kind of sensory stimuli we are bound to be exposed to. This includes television, radio, bright lights, billboards, and the ongoing addiction to social media, where people can't seem to stop binging on endless videos, memes, and pictures. All these things we take in constantly cause our sensory systems to be affected in one way or another. Have you ever been exposed to a disturbing video and then noticed that you couldn't seem to brush it off or get it out of your mind, even days later? It's even worse when you read or watch challenging or emotionally charged content just before you fall asleep. Your subconscious mind holds onto that content and before you know it, your mind is racing and you may even experience nightmares. Neither is great for helping you get to sleep for that essential physical rest. Taking a break from sensory stimuli helps your mind free itself from constant triggers and mental exhaustion. It's important to be mindful of your habits when it comes to what you expose your brain to, because what you take in will either drain or strengthen you.

7. **Creative Rest:** Creative rest is all about filling your life with creativity and enjoying the beauty of nature. This type of rest helps you to get into a different gear and appreciate the beauty all around you. Life shouldn't just be all about work, work, and work. Everyone needs to make some time for a little introspection, and it doesn't need to feel intimidating. We often talk about introspection in terms of focusing on our failings or what we need to do better, but it also has to do with your relationships, personal life, and work life. Setting time aside to think about how these aspects are going for you can open up a fresh perspective. You can also encourage creative rest by adding visually appealing art and decorations to your personal and work

spaces. Choose colors and designs that help you feel relaxed whenever you are in those decorated spaces. Incorporate creativity in your relationships by making room for adventure and spontaneity. When you experience life in this way with others, it becomes easier to form lasting bonds, so you'll never have to worry about whether you're doing enough to keep things fresh. All of this contributes to a life that is not constantly plagued by worry and self-doubt. Finding ways to add color and beauty to your surroundings and everyday life helps you to enjoy creative rest. It's tiring to live a life that has you following the same routine that doesn't satisfy or motivate you. Make creative rest a habit by incorporating creativity into every aspect of your life. With time, you'll see your quality of life improving as your stress and anxiety levels lessen.

Now that we have unpacked what the seven different types of rest are and why they are important, let's unpack the myriad benefits of making sure you're getting enough of each one.

The Myriad Benefits of Rest

The effects of rest deprivation will vary from person to person, and some people seem to be able to function a little better on less sleep than others. However, there can be no doubt that stress and chronic burnout become inevitable at some point in the cycle, and a person's performance at home, school, work, and everywhere else will decline over time. Let's unpack more of the detailed benefits that come from maintaining a lifestyle where rest is a priority:

- **Improves physical health:** When you sleep, that's when your body gets a chance to repair and refresh without interruptions. That means that after adequate rest, your body's functions will be at their best, such as being able to digest and process food and the nutrients you're taking in, as well as recovering from injury or anything strenuous that you put your body through regularly. Have you ever noticed that your heart beats faster when you are doing something that requires more physical energy? It also beats fast when you are anxious about something. However, during your sleep time, your heart starts to beat slower, which allows your blood pressure to also reduce. Being exposed to prolonged periods of high blood pressure may eventually lead to health risks, such as developing chronic high blood pressure, stroke, and heart disease. Sleep also allows you to regulate your eating frequency. I'm sure you have noticed that when people are struggling to get enough sleep each night, they tend to grab anything they can get their hands on for meals and are more prone to binging on unhealthy food. That means, if you are constantly sleep-deprived, you're prone to overeating and gaining excess weight, which can cause a whole host of other problems down the road. In addition to adequate sleep, relaxing activities such as yoga and stretching exercises or massages can help you to destress and produce less stress cortisol for improved overall well-being.

- **Great energy and a pleasant aura:** Nobody likes to be around someone who is moody all the time or who lashes out at others whenever they're in a bad mood. When people are deprived of rest, it makes them very irritable and easily annoyed. They become very unpleasant to be around, and this may lead to an inability to build rapport and good connections with others. However, when you get enough rest, you are better able to emotionally regulate yourself and be fully conscious of the impact of your actions. This self-awareness helps you to be intentional about radiating positive energy wherever you go, leading to greater satisfaction with the quality of your life experiences. It's hard to be positive and enjoy the company of other people when you can barely hold yourself together due to fatigue. If you notice that your mood has been hitting rock bottom and you are pushing people away, it may be worth considering whether a nap is what you need to press that reset button and restore harmony and tranquility to your energy and interactions.

- **Improves quality of communication with others:** The brain is unable to think clearly or organize ideas well when it's fatigued. This is why people who haven't had much rest tend to behave in unreasonable ways and communicate poorly, and this can damage the quality of their relationships or work. You are likely to sound more dismissive or passive in your communication when your mind is not functioning at its highest potential. When you're affected by a lack of rest, it's important to delay any important conversations to a later time after you have managed to make up for that lost rest if you want to avoid saying something you didn't mean, which could jeopardize the relationship. You will be more alert and attentive to what someone is saying to you if you are well-rested. Good communication will improve your relationships and open doors for opportunities as you build a positive reputation in every area of your life. On the other hand, there is always a price to pay for poor communication, and repairing a damaged relationship due to poor communication can take some time, depending on the circumstances. Adequate rest can enhance your cognitive skills, such as enhancing your memory, and keep you aware of everything happening in your life.

- **Enhances concentration and better productivity:** When someone hasn't had enough rest, you can see it in the quality of their work, and it becomes harder and harder to foster creativity and achieve the same level of productivity and success as when they began. When your productivity levels fall because you can't keep up with your daily goals and responsibilities, you are likely to experience greater dissatisfaction with your life, as your self-actualization needs are not being met, either. Sometimes the lack of productivity can be so bad that you are unable to make enough money to provide for yourself or your family. This is a worst-case scenario, but without proper care and attention to rest deficits, it is a possibility for anyone. Without rest, you won't be able to perform at work, and that means an employer may choose to replace you. Whatever your situation, it is possible to plan ahead and prioritize rest time wherever you have the opportunity. For instance, people who have to be at work early in the morning need to avoid staying up late, as this can make it hard for them to be ready for the next day's work and excel in what they do. Getting enough rest guarantees that you will have sufficient energy for the day, and this helps you make fewer mistakes because your mind will be fully alert and working at its best. It's hard to think outside the box and generate new ideas when you can barely concentrate and stay awake; that is why rest is essential for maintaining your creativity and enhancing your overall performance in every aspect of your life. Ultimately, people who prioritize holistic rest tend to enjoy their lives more because of a great work-life balance. To them, life is not just about all work and no play. Life is more about working to live instead of living to work, day in and day out.

- **Substantially slows down the aging process:** Your body works extra hard when you are active and up and about. Since sleeping also gives your heart the chance to get some rest, healthier sleep habits equals a healthier heart, and your body will be able to function better compared to someone who is bombarded with fatigue every single day. Since cell renewal and body rebuilding take place when we are resting, it is no exaggeration to say that people who get more rest tend to age much slower than those who hardly rest.

- **Protects your mental health and increases your ability to make better decisions:** A lack of sensory rest can leave your mind feeling extra fatigued and clouded, with lots of unprocessed information that may impair your judgment or interfere with your decision-making powers. If your mind is constantly exposed to many kinds of sensory stimuli, good and bad, that will affect the kind of person you grow to become. For instance, consider how easy access to social media has led to many mental health issues, as people strive to reach out for unrealistic beauty, fame, and wealth ideals that are portrayed by prominent and popular figures. It's important to give yourself a break from the constant scrolling, because social media addiction creates pressure that causes people to forget what matters and tempts them to chase after views and likes. When this happens, people lose sight of what really provides value in their lives, like their true relationships, and instead they get sucked into a cycle of unhealthy and unrealistic expectations for themselves. On the other hand, people who practice discipline and good habits around what they allow their minds to be exposed to tend to have better mental health, as well as the intelligence to make sound life decisions. Be aware of how your relationships and habits affect you and lean in toward the ones which feed you positive energy instead of toxicity. No one needs to be weighed down by others' negativity.

At the end of the day, there is no doubt that a life built from a foundation of proper rest in all its forms yields endless benefits that will continue for as long as you maintain those healthy habits. To ensure that you get the most out of these benefits, let's take some time to explore in-depth each type of rest. This way, you will understand how to practically incorporate all these kinds of rest into your daily routine. Embracing this evolved way of living will help you to finally say goodbye to the endless struggle of barely getting by and say a big long-awaited hello to a life free from chronic burnout and stress for good.

Chapter 3:

Physical Rest

There is nothing so satisfying as snuggling up in your bed after a long day of hard work and stress. It's that one thing we all look forward to, but it's certainly not always easy or guaranteed. The tremendous number of responsibilities many of us have on our shoulders sometimes makes it hard to get enough physical rest. Nevertheless, with a little more tweaking of your daily routine, it's possible to carve out some time for yourself to get to sleep earlier than usual, or at least get an hour to nap during the day to recharge. People who have more physical rest tend to function a lot better than those who are deprived of it. There is no way you can overcome stress and burnout if your body is constantly physically drained. Therefore, to ensure that you optimize your physical rest, be open and explore the many different options and strategies out there to help you make the most of the time you have for recharging your body.

Most people who end up hitting the wall of burnout fail to see the signs that led up to that point. In this way, it's kind of like being struck by lightning, and the surprise and confusion can only add to the mounting pressures of chronic stress. It takes a lot more effort to climb out of a state of burnout than it does to monitor your health so that you recognize the signs of fatigue before they mature into that catastrophic status where energy is depleted. This is why it is important for anyone and everyone to reflect on the quality of their lives, even when things seem like they are running smoothly. You can avoid having to deal with chronic stress and burnout and avoid disappointment by putting preventative measures in place now, while you are aware of your situation and stress levels. This is one responsibility that is worth taking on so that you don't end up in a place where life just feels like too much.

Chronic stress is an indication that your life is spiraling out of control, so it will benefit you immensely if you rearrange everything on your schedule, including your priorities. We live in a society where everyone is used to being busy, but motion doesn't mean that you are making progress in the direction you wish to go in. You must carefully consider what your goals are and where you want to expend your energy, because we all only get a certain amount before we need to rest and recharge. Wisdom is knowing where to spend that energy so that by the time you do get tired, most of what's urgent and important to you has already been sorted out.

The first step in preventing physical fatigue is to examine your lifestyle and your daily activities. You can eliminate those which cost you a lot of time and energy without sufficient reward or payoff regarding what's relevant to you. Sometimes we take on the burden of doing things the hard way instead of identifying areas where we can work smarter instead of harder. This happens for many reasons, one of which is deferring to the way things have always been done. Look at ways to improve efficiency, even if it means experimenting. The payoff could be that you accomplish more with less energy, which will be worth your time. For instance, with the advancement of technology in our day and age, there are many things people used to do manually that they can now do using machines and other automated systems. You can order your groceries or hire cleaning services online instead of putting in the work yourself. There is software available to automate laborious tasks like calculating taxes or coordinating work meetings.

To really kill two birds with one stone, consider what we call "bundling." You can bundle healthy physical exercise together with your daily chores. This can make the work more enjoyable as you activate those feel-good hormones. An example of how you can bundle exercise with chores is when you get your daily steps in while taking your dog for a 30-minute walk. Knowing that you are streamlining your work can give you something to look forward to, which in turn gives you more energy and motivation to undergo whatever current challenges you are facing.

Take some time to observe and write down which times of the day you are usually most active and filled with energy. Use those times when your energy is at its peak by scheduling those laborious physical duties. That way, you're not slogging through a task when your body is at a low energy point. The problems and overwhelming stress come when you try to force yourself to do tiring things when your energy levels are low. Forcing yourself to work during the times when your body is not ready for it makes your stress cortisol levels rise, and this can lead to substandard work. It's better to be accepting of your energy patterns and learn to respect what your body needs, when it needs it. For instance, if you notice that you are a night person and have trouble falling asleep at a reasonable time, avoid being on screens late at night to encourage better quality sleep. If you have to start work in the mornings, ensure that you've prepared for your day the night before so you're not scrambling to get things ready right before leaving. This will help you if you need lots of time to properly wake up. If you've got your clothes laid out already and your work things organized, you can use that morning time to wake up without stress, maybe enjoying a cup of coffee outside in the sunshine. The times when your energy is at its lowest is when you should take the rest that you need.

The body has an incredible ability to adjust to what we train it to get used to. Take training yourself to wake up at the same time every morning, for example. For the first few days, your mind will heavily rely on your alarm clock. However, as time goes by and you keep waking up at that time, your mind eventually registers that the time you have been waking up is the standard time to wake up. After a while, you'll notice that you start to naturally wake up at the designated time, even without an alarm clock. You've trained your mind and body, and now you're accustomed to that routine. When you reach this stage, it's time for you to celebrate, because even if you rest for just a few hours, your body will still wake you up at that same time, and you won't feel drained. The hardest part is the first few days before your mind is used to waking up at that time. All this changes because biologically, the brain starts to develop a neurological network that supports the act of you waking up at the time when you consistently choose to wake up. Before those neurological pathways formed, you were defaulting to your old patterns of inconsistent sleep. But the moment it becomes a habit, your brain turns the act of waking up at a certain time into an automatic response, as it follows the existing neurological pathways for that habit. This explains why you can become addicted to fatigue. If that pattern is not disrupted, you end up reinforcing the habit of being fatigued all the time. That's why it's important to disrupt any pattern of fatigue you might be noticing each day by retraining your brain to either rest or be active at particular times. After a while, that new routine will become automatic.

Many people try to overcome physical fatigue by just sleeping a lot more, but I'm sure you've noticed how that, too, can be futile. You might wonder, why am I feeling drained even after letting myself sleep in? If that's not the answer, what am I supposed to do to effectively end such fatigue?

Before treating any illness or solving any problem, it's important to have a correct diagnosis of the underlying problem and why it's there in the first place. Identifying the signs and symptoms of that problem helps us understand the root issue, and this will tell us which remedy to apply to fix things. Having said that, burnout and chronic stress are conditions partly caused by a lack of physical rest. That means, before the problem matures into its full-blown state, there must be signs and symptoms that should help us understand that our bodies and minds are in desperate need of physical rest. Let's take a look at the common signs and symptoms of physical rest deprivation.

Signs That You Desperately Need Physical Rest

When it comes to babies, it's easy for mothers to notice when their little ones need some rest. The babies simply cry… *a lot*. If you have fed the baby and their diaper is clean, then there is seldom any other reason why the baby might have a meltdown other than the need for rest. Without enough rest, babies and toddlers can give you a hard time, even to the point where you feel like crying yourself! It's easy for us to notice these signs and symptoms with our young ones, but when it comes to adults, sometimes we take our signs and symptoms lightly because of the belief that we don't deserve to rest until everything is checked off our to-do lists. However, that belief seldom ever makes things better; all it does is move you farther away from meeting your needs and before you know it, many problems are piling up in your life. We adults need rest, too. We need it every single day, and it should never be a "Once in a while, I get good sleep" kind of thing. No. You have to look after yourself and not let these obligations and ingrained beliefs get in the way of prioritizing your own well-being. So, how can you identify as an adult the signs indicating that you are in urgent need of physical rest? Let's have a look at some of the common symptoms:

- **Feeling uninterested and lacking energy for your daily activities:** It's okay to feel tired and unmotivated to do your daily activities once in a while. However, constantly feeling that way may be an indication that your body is in desperate need of rest and recharging.

- **Constantly feeling like you need to sleep for hours and just be left alone:** We have all reached that point of physical exhaustion at some point in our lives, where we just want to be left alone to binge on sleep for as long as we want. If this becomes a constant feeling, then it may indicate that you are rest deprived.

- **Insistent body aches**: When the body is exhausted, it's common for people to start experiencing aches and pains. You'll feel it in your muscles, and doing normal things like running or lifting weights can become a challenge.

- **Heavy reliance on substances to stay awake or active:** There are lots of good supplements available to keep your body energized, but they are not always people's first choice next to less healthy and more readily available options. These include stimulants like caffeine and energy drinks. Heavily relying on these substances just to be able to function is a clear indication of a serious need for rest and recharging.

- **Forgetting things easily and struggling to focus:** When we are rest deprived, it becomes hard to focus on much of anything. Our attention becomes very limited, and even remembering things can become a challenge.

- **Lack of creativity:** When your body is exhausted, you start operating in survival mode instead of thinking outside the box and being able to solve problems creatively. Your life becomes confined to the same mundane routine without any space to pursue creative or enriching pastimes.

- **Being irritable and prone to regular mood swings:** Just as babies have meltdowns when they are tired, adults also have mood changes when they are battling with fatigue. This is seen in being constantly on edge, lashing out at people, taking things personally, and being unable to think rationally. As a result of mood swings, people can end up acting in irrational ways.

- **Getting sick frequently:** Due to a weakened immune system because of inadequate rest, your body starts having a harder time warding off illness. As a result, you may end up getting ill or feeling unwell without understanding clearly what the problem is.

- **Looking unhealthy:** Noticeable signs of fatigue start to show up on the body whenever you're exhausted beyond what you can bear. These signs can range from having red eyes and looking pale to gaining or losing weight due to stress and worsened eating patterns. You lose the "glow" people speak about when someone is looking healthy and doing well.

What's even scarier than all these signs is when you start to notice that you are losing touch with yourself and merely spending most of your time completing one task after another. You might become disconnected from your dreams and the things that used to matter to you as you invest more of your time fulfilling your role at work and at home. If you're noticing this happening to you, it's important that you take the time to declutter your life, make room for rest, and reconnect with your heart's dreams. To get you back in that gear where you are physically fit, well rested, and ready to attend to your life's purpose with wholehearted devotion, let's unpack some simple tips for ways you can optimize your rest.

How to Optimize Your Physical Rest

Optimizing your rest means more than resorting to sleep as a solution to end your physical fatigue. There are many other physical things you can do to make your rest efficient and rewarding. You certainly don't want to wake up after a long nap still feeling tired, so here are some ways to ensure that your body is well-rested:

- **Breathing exercises:** When we are exhausted, our breathing patterns become interrupted. To restore your breathing rate to a good pace, you can do deep breathing exercises. To do breathing exercises, all you have to do is find a comfortable place to recline. Next, take some time to inhale as much air as you can through your nose. Watch your belly rise as you fill your lungs with air. Then slowly start to exhale some air through your nose. Doing this for at least five to ten minutes helps to ease stress and get your body into a relaxed state. Deep breathing is also helpful when you feel anxious or overwhelmed, as it gives your body the chance to regain composure and stabilize your nervous system.

- **Massage therapy:** You work hard constantly fending for others and making sure everyone else is okay. Why is it that we sometimes feel bad about giving ourselves a special treat by going on a spa date? Consider refreshing your body by getting a professional deep massage, if funds permit. With the advancements in technology, you still have access to that much-needed massage therapy, even if you can't afford a professional. If you go to the Google Play Store or App Store, there are many apps you can find after typing in "massage therapy" that will teach you great massage techniques that you can do yourself. Others require someone else to administer the massage to you, and that's okay because you can use that as an opportunity to bond with your loved ones! Set aside at least 30 minutes every single week just to give yourself that body treatment. Your body will most certainly thank you.

- **Switch off from the rest of the world and be immersed in your own world:** It's hard to get good rest if people are constantly buzzing your phone and others are demanding your time and physical presence. That's why it's important to inform the people you live with of your rest times so that your sleep won't be interrupted. Unplug from your noisy world and resist the temptation to constantly use your electronic devices. Screens emit blue light, which inhibits the production of melatonin—a sleep-inducing hormone. This is why you should make it a habit to avoid using electronics and silence your notifications or put your phone in airplane mode just before bedtime to promote good sleep and prevent eye strain.

- **Stretching exercises:** As discussed earlier in this book, stretching exercises come in handy when your body needs more than sleep. Your muscles are constantly under tension and becoming tired. Taking time to stretch through things like aerobics, yoga, or Tai Chi helps the body's muscles to regain stamina. Doing stretching exercises for at least 10 minutes a day just after waking up and right after work can help reduce your exhaustion levels. If you are at work, you can also use stretching exercises as an icebreaker in meetings before diving into things that require high levels of concentration from your team. Stretching exercises are well known for enhancing concentration and giving the body the boost of energy it needs during those sluggish times of the day, like just after lunch.

- **Listen to music before bed:** Have you ever wondered what it is about music that makes us love it so much that we can't live without it? Music stimulates feel-good hormones in our bodies, such as dopamine and oxytocin. Sometimes physical fatigue is worsened by the state of your mind. If you don't feel good, you feel drained. Using both music and physical rest can help improve the quality of your rest time. When you're trying to get some rest, it's best to choose slow, peaceful jams rather than upbeat songs. Instrumental music with nature or rain sounds is very soothing and can help you to relax physically, too.

- **Take a bath with bath salts:** Before going to bed, consider taking a nice hot bath. Adding bath salts can help your body to become even more relaxed. However, if you don't have bath salts, consider taking your bath whilst listening to music that makes you feel great and that fills your mind with pleasant thoughts.

- **Snuggle with a novel or watch your favorite shows while resting on a couch:** There are many ways to get your body physically relaxed. Grabbing a healthy smoothie and a book to read, or just watching television whilst relaxing are other ways to give your mind rest. When you make the time to do things like this regularly, you'll no longer feel the need to sleep extra long, as your body will already be physically rested.

- **Drink relaxing herbal teas before you sleep:** Herbal teas have powerful properties that ease stress and help your body to relax in ways that complement your sleep. There are several common teas worth trying out that are time-tested and well-loved for their relaxation benefits, including chamomile, peppermint, lavender, and passionflower tea. Having a cup just before bed will help you to sleep soundly. They are also helpful for people who struggle with insomnia and nightmares. They support your body to sleep deeply, which helps to put your mind at ease and allows your body to rest well without interruption. They are also popular for their help in reducing stress and anxiety problems. Ultimately, these healthy herbal drinks are considered extremely helpful in boosting the immune system and warding off many body ailments. Use herbal teas along with drinking lots of water and reducing your alcohol intake to encourage the best rest of your life.

- **Dim the lights and lower the noise:** Bright lights and loud noise make it almost impossible for your body to switch off and go into a relaxed mode. It's always good to either switch your lights off before bed or dim them, as this will help improve your sleep quality. Most bright artificial lights are also known to emit blue light, which affects the production of melatonin in your body. This is why you might have noticed that every time you try to sleep with the lights on, it is hard to fall asleep. If you do sleep, you might notice that sometimes your sleep is shortened or disrupted.

- **Find a comfortable bed that doesn't cause neck or back pains:** It's pointless to focus on all these different behavioral changes if an uncomfortable bed is the underlying culprit causing poor sleep. Everyone's preference is a little different, but it's worth taking the time to find a bed that supports your body correctly and promotes good rest. Having a good quality mattress or using a weighted blanket may improve your comfort level and the quality of your sleep.

- **Time block:** One of the most important strategies to incorporate into your daily routine is to allow your body to get some physical or mental rest not only at bedtime but also at intervals throughout the day. You can accomplish this by time blocking. This is when you split up your day into sections and devote each time slot to completing a specific task without interruptions. For instance, you can choose to use the first three hours of your day to complete your most difficult tasks. As soon as that three-hour time block is over, reward yourself with at least 30 minutes of rest or less strenuous physical or mental activity. Doing this will help you avoid overworking to the point that your body rebels on you and shuts down with fatigue. As a bonus, knowing that your schedule is balanced in this way gives you peace of mind. Rearrange your routine so that rest is a priority in your schedule, and you'll finally achieve a life free of chronic stress and impending burnout.

Now that we have explored in depth how you can maximize your physical rest, it's time that we explore how you can also balance that physical rest with mental rest. As we now know, sometimes even extra physical rest is not enough to recharge if you're dealing with burnout.. Therefore, let's dive into the next chapter and explore how you can start treating your mind with the same level of care and attention you give to your body. After all, a happy mind sure does lead to a happy life!

Chapter 4:

Mental Rest

Can we all agree on the fact that mental rest is a fundamental human need and not a luxury? Many people believe that physical rest is all the rest you need while disregarding the fact that you can physically rest but still feel mentally drained and exhausted. That alone is evidence that we need more than just physical rest. We thrive only when we also allow ourselves to get mental rest. Do you ever feel like your mind is constantly bombarding you with racing thoughts? You may even find yourself sighing at the level of activity transpiring in your brain. This is the case for many of us—we are always thinking and processing things mentally, and all of that requires energy. Making decisions also requires energy, which is why creating a lifestyle with a streamlined daily routine helps to prevent what is known as *decision fatigue*. Once you repeat a habit many times, your brain begins to rely on the neural pathways you've formed, and that habit is then automatically carried out. That means the more regular habits you maintain, the less mental strain you will experience from having to make those independent decisions all the time. Instead, your brain will just automatically prompt you to execute the habit seamlessly.

Many things can cause mental exhaustion. Let's have a look at some of the common causes of mental strain and fatigue.

Work-related causes:

- **Job dissatisfaction:** The joy of landing your dream job is beyond surreal. Now, imagine having to go to a job every single day that you don't even like. As people, we feel more satisfied with our lives when we receive growth and advancement in exchange for the efforts we put in at work. If you are stuck in a job that doesn't allow room to grow, it can take a lot out of you just to get out of bed and drag yourself to the office. Instead of something you look forward to, a job you are dissatisfied with is bound to feel like a burden. If you have a demanding job that requires you to work long hours without fair compensation, this too can be a major cause of mental exhaustion. Even if you are offered a generous salary, working crazy long hours is bound to have a negative impact on your mental health. Establishing a work-life balance is important, but sometimes your job won't allow that. This is when you have to take the initiative and figure out how to fix your situation, regardless of how challenging that task might seem.

- **Stress due to worrying about finances or costs of living:** Taking care of your daily needs is not child's play. It requires a commitment to your job or whatever source of income you employ; otherwise, problems just start to pile up. Without enough income, you will be unable to provide for your basic needs, including food, water, shelter, clothing, transport, and so on. Without job security, stress and worry over money is a daily struggle, since you're constantly wondering if you're going to have a job tomorrow, next week, or next month. All the "what ifs" only add to this anxiety. *What if I can't pay my bills on time? What if I can't feed my kids?* Having more liabilities than assets is also a road that leads to financial problems, including overwhelming debt, struggling to get approved for loans, or becoming dependent on others for your survival needs. Many people are struggling and living paycheck to paycheck, and if they can't break this cycle, there will be no room for joy or life satisfaction.

- **Dealing with difficult people:** People have different personalities, making them either pleasant to be around and interact with or disagreeable in many social situations. Some people who are struggling with their lives choose to project their pain and frustration onto others, and this can even turn toxic. Everyone gets in moods and is unpleasant from time to time, though that is why we all need to be mindful of the energy we are exuding in our daily interactions with others. Good communication is impeded when someone you are talking to fails to show signs of being sincerely engaged in what you are saying or chooses to deliberately dismiss your words. Effective communication is also disrupted when someone fails to acknowledge when they are at fault and apologize for their mistakes. It can be mentally exhausting to have to deal with a defensive person who hardly ever self-reflects and admits when they are wrong.

Other causes:

- **Parenting:** One of the best things in life is experiencing the joys of having a baby. It often brings unparalleled joy and so much brightness to a parent's life. Nevertheless, there is also a difficult side to parenting that involves challenges like losing sleep or being woken up throughout the night to tend to the child. And it certainly doesn't stop anytime soon! Children at every stage require love and patience from their parents, and this means a lot of stress and worry is in store. This can all become overwhelming, and if you are a parent, you know that finding ways to put your mind at ease as often as possible is a must in order to maintain good mental health and energy levels.

- **Recurring relationship problems:** Relationships can be a major source of stress and mental fatigue, especially when there are unresolved issues stewing right beneath the surface. When there is a poor connection between people, communication suffers and misunderstandings can become commonplace. It's never comfortable to feel like you have to walk on eggshells around someone you care about, and it can feel impossible to just be yourself. This is how relationships deteriorate, and the end result is either a complete dissolution or worse—toxicity and abuse is allowed to grow where there was once love and compassion. Ruminating on past mistakes and hurts is also one of the most common causes of mental exhaustion. It's tiring to have to leave a situation carrying the burden of a grudge against someone. It not only affects your mental health but your physical well-being, too. The inability to let go of the past and bitterness often go hand-in-hand, making it hard for someone who is holding onto the past to move on and enjoy life with a healthy mindset. A person with this emotional addiction cycle is constantly plagued by painful memories or flashbacks of what hurt them. When this is allowed to go on unchecked, nothing is resolved and instead, the situation tends to get worse and worse.

- **Chronic illness**: We all get sick once in a while, but most of the time, this is followed by a natural recovery to full strength. However, the battle of dealing with a chronic illness such as cancer, diabetes, arthritis, heart disease, and so forth can take a much larger toll on your mental health. On top of all the common daily struggles we all have to bear, people battling with chronic illnesses have the added challenge of managing their health and the exorbitant costs that may come with it. It's important that those close to the sufferer practice empathy and find ways to be supportive, however it may be needed.

- **Grief**: Losing a loved one can be emotionally, mentally, and physically straining, as one must deal with the void left behind where there was once love and warmth. For instance, if you lost a husband or wife, it can be very difficult to cope with that loss not only because you miss them and love them but also because you might have to take over the responsibilities they used to carry. Raising a child as a single parent after the other parent has died is very strenuous. If proper self-care strategies aren't put in place, the loss of a loved one can even lead to mental health problems such as depression and Post Traumatic Stress Disorder (PTSD).

The above examples are only the tip of the iceberg, as I'm sure many other examples of what causes mental strain are surfacing in your mind. Armed with the knowledge that all these things can have a negative impact on our mental health, why do we still allow ourselves to live lives that aren't fruitful for our mental health?

There are many reasons why people may continue to go down the path of mentally straining themselves, either knowingly or unknowingly, and one of them is being a perfectionist—meaning you don't rest until everything is "Perfect." This personality trait drives those who have it to impose unreasonable expectations on themselves and others, and this, too, results in chronic stress. Another reason why people don't rest is because they assume that a good night's sleep is all they need to fix it. As we already went over in previous chapters, sleeping is only one part of rest; there are many other forms of rest that are fundamental to a healthy and balanced life. We can all empathize with the desire to hand down a better life to our kids than what we had ourselves, and this is a common reason behind someone pushing themselves beyond their limits, which only ends in burnout and mental health issues. To help us discover ways we can effectively incorporate and prioritize mental rest in our lives, let's take a look at the following section. Read on for practical strategies that you can use to foster a better work-life balance.

Pragmatic Tips to Practice Mental Rest

At work:
- **Respectfully offer suggestions at work for ways to improve conditions:** One of the main causes of stress and anxiety in adult years is working in a toxic job environment. Since this is somewhere you will inevitably spend a lot of time, it's important that you actively contribute to creating a positive atmosphere that is conducive to working in peace and harmony. The mistake many people make is just complaining about their work situation without directly addressing the matter in a proactive way. Speak with your boss or appropriate higher-ups and offer a detailed

solution for how things can improve; this way, you will be one step closer to creating a pleasant and motivating work environment.

- **Create a new routine with scheduled breaks:** The drive to get things done as quickly as possible sometimes gets in the way of our mental health. It is possible to be a high achiever without compromising your mental well-being. One way to do this is to revise your daily routine and ensure that your timetable has scheduled short breaks that are evenly distributed throughout your day to help you maintain your mental stamina. During those breaks, try to get a change of scenery. This means, instead of spending your break in the same place where you are working, you should visit another room or go outside. This will help refresh your mind and rejuvenate your energy levels.

- **Set attainable daily goals:** There is more you can achieve by diligently taking small steps toward a big goal compared to trying to do a million things all at once. Burnout strikes when someone tries to do many things at the same time without the mental capacity to take on such tremendous responsibility. There is a meme out there about the one who is slow and steady being the one who wins the race over the fast and furious one who is bound to crash. The lesson here is to break down your annual, monthly, or weekly goals into small, attainable tasks. As you consistently achieve your daily goals, you will be working through your to-do list at a pace that is sustainable.

- **Practice assertively saying "No" when you need to:** Everyone has a limit to the amount of information they can process at a time. Anything beyond that limit becomes information overload. Learning how much you can take helps you to plan and create a strategy for getting the job done. Once you understand yourself, it's important to draw the line and make it known to those around you when you are unable to take on anything extra. Effective communication and practicing delegation will help ensure that you don't end up taking on too many responsibilities.

For the rest of life:

- **Exercise and mindfulness meditation:** Exercising is a great way to alleviate stress and maintain a healthy body, and that includes your mind, too. If you are constantly feeling sluggish and mentally challenged, starting or ending your day with a set of aerobic exercises can help to increase your blood flow and thus make more oxygen available to your brain. This will help you to be more alert and perform at your best.

- **Take an extended vacation with loved ones:** Sometimes a big, long-awaited vacation can be the answer to ending chronic fatigue. A vacation can allow you to gain perspective, as you get a chance to look at your life differently and switch off from the autopilot that may have been taking over. Journaling, going for long walks, eating great food, meeting new people, exploring tourist sites, and exercising are all amazing ways to recoup your mental stamina while you are on vacation.

- **Make it a habit to appreciate your efforts and what you achieve:** The older we get, the more likely we are to take our efforts for granted. At some point, we start to expect so much from ourselves without appreciating just how much we are already doing. This shouldn't be the case. It's important to recognize that you are working hard so that you don't downplay the toll it's taking on you. A little self-respect will go a long way when it comes to how others perceive you as well. When you appreciate yourself, this brings healing to your weary soul and becomes a form of self-motivation that can give you the strength to keep pushing.

- **Temporarily unplug from social media:** Social media can be mentally draining, especially when you are constantly exposed to disturbing or emotionally charged content. With the growth in popularity of social media nowadays, people are using it as a platform to showcase their achievements or portray a fictional, perfect life that they don't have in reality. As you watch this stuff routinely, you might not be able to discern between what's fact and what's fiction. As a result, you might end up comparing yourself with others and feeling depressed about your life. This causes mental unrest, and the only way to avoid this is by intentionally controlling your algorithms on social media and taking some time to unplug from it.

- **Drink relaxing herbal teas:** Herbal teas have tremendous cognitive benefits, as they are jam-packed with nutrients that support brain function. Examples of teas you can try to calm your mind and promote good memory include hibiscus, cinnamon, chamomile, spearmint, green teas, and licorice. Taking a hot cup of any of those teas on a stressful day or just before bedtime will help massage and recharge your mind and body.

- **Forgive and make amends with the past:** Holding onto past hurts and harboring resentment makes it hard for your mental health to thrive. It takes energy to hold on to negative emotions, and thus those negative emotions have to be released through intentionally choosing to forgive and forget. Allowing healing and growth to take place in broken relationships helps you to rest from all the internal turmoil of dealing with feuds and holding onto bitterness.

- **Relaxation techniques:** Your mind is usually active, and sometimes the only way to get it into a relaxed mode is to try out relaxation techniques. These include doing things like aromatherapy, yoga, Tai Chi, self-hypnosis, guided meditation, and massages. Set aside time in your schedule to incorporate these relaxation activities so that you can get the deep rest your mind needs. Sometimes just having time to think and reflect on all the beautiful things in your life can help you to gain perspective and shift from feeling frustrated to being grateful and more content with your life.

- **Listening to calm music:** Soft, soothing music that makes you feel happy gives you that feeling because music releases a feel-good hormone known as dopamine. This is why you might have noticed that your mood can radically change the moment you listen to music that speaks to you. Doing this especially when you are hyper-stressed or struggling to sleep can help lower cortisol levels and increase melatonin production—a sleep hormone.

- **Build a reliable support structure:** Being alone and feeling lonely can exacerbate stress and mental fatigue. Loving relationships help us feel much better, and being around people who care about us can expose us to potential ideas and solutions that can help to resolve any issues we might be facing. Try to cultivate a strong relationship with at least three friends or family members with whom you can build a mutually supportive connection. Sometimes just going about the daily tasks of adulthood without having the refreshing presence of people who deeply care about us can be the cause of mental exhaustion. Great relationships are known to trigger the production of a feel-good hormone called oxytocin.

- **Prioritize your "Me" time:** When you enter the parenting and adulthood stage, it's highly likely that you will have times when you forget that there is life beyond being a mother or father. You are also an individual who has personal needs and a unique identity outside all those other roles. This lack of mindfulness of what you need as an individual can be one of the reasons why your life gets so immersed in fulfilling your roles while you forget about yourself. This inevitably leads to mental exhaustion, as your mind will soon start to scream for attention. There is only so much you can pour out from a cup that isn't being replenished. What I mean by this is: For you to continue to be at your best in all the other areas of your life, it's of paramount importance that you set aside time to rejuvenate yourself by nourishing your mental health. Set aside some time each day to tend to any mental needs you might have. Perhaps you are lacking motivation and this is causing you to feel mentally drained. Perhaps just taking a break to read a good book or take a walk in nature is what you need. Or maybe you need to talk to a loved one who makes your spirit feel alive again. If you let others know about your personal time, it will help them to be more supportive of your needs.

- **Maintain a healthy diet:** There are many foods that help to keep the mind active and functioning at its best. Examples of these foods include things like dark chocolate, salmon, avocadoes, blueberries, turmeric, eggs, kale, and many other nutritious foods. Dark chocolate is known to improve cognitive brain function by increasing blood flow to the brain. It is also rich in antioxidants which help to reduce oxidative stress. Salmon is excellent for reducing brain fog and increasing your memory quality because of the effect of omega-3 fatty acids that are packed in it. Avocadoes, kale, and blueberries are rich in vitamin K, which helps to improve concentration and memory. Turmeric is an excellent agent in helping to boost oxygen intake to the brain, which in turn makes you more mentally awake and alert. Eggs contain an essential nutrient called choline which is helpful for brain development (Super Nutritious, 2022).

Any of the above suggestions can make a world of difference in optimizing your mental health. It's important that you take some time to analyze which strategy will work best for your lifestyle and start implementing it as soon as possible. When it comes to change, your mind might resist at first because of the convenience of resorting to what's already familiar. This is why you have to be very intentional about defeating your old mindset and allowing a new growth mindset to develop. Your mental well-being will be refreshed if you get enough rest. As each week comes to an end, always ask yourself if you have looked after your mental health. Taking even just 30 minutes to rejuvenate your mental health is better than doing nothing at all.

Another form of rest that is very similar to mental rest is emotional rest. Both types of rest can be practiced simultaneously. Let's dive into the next chapter to explore ways in which you can finally make emotional rest a practical part of your life.

Chapter 5:

Emotional Rest

One of the prominent signs of burnout and stress is when you start to see signs of emotional exhaustion. This is when you plunge into an emotional dip—a phase where you feel like your emotions are out of control and you can't regulate your moods. Your mind starts to feel foggy, and getting things done becomes harder than before. The usual day-to-day tasks and responsibilities that you usually carry with ease become burdensome to you, and along with this kind of exhaustion comes procrastination. Our productivity is directly impacted by our emotional state, so it's important to stay aware of your emotional health and keep track of the patterns you're experiencing if they're leading you to that edge of chronic burnout. With this awareness, you can begin to work toward a way out. After reading this chapter, you'll have a guide to help you climb out of emotional exhaustion and find rest.

As an adult with a busy life filled with countless daily duties, it's easy to consider your emotional health as a last priority. It seems like physical and mental rest are way more important at first, but this is not the case at all. Emotions are energy, and our emotions can be changed through motion. This means that for you to move away from an emotional state of being exhausted or drained, you'll need to get in motion and change your physiology. A radical change in your physiological state will result in a radical change in your emotional state.

There are obvious signs of emotional exhaustion that you can see through someone's body language and demeanor. People who are battling with emotional fatigue tend to show signs like being absent-minded and apathetic or looking demotivated, with noticeably decreased productivity. Other signs include forgetting things easily, complaining a lot, sleeping a lot, having poor eating habits, a lack of enthusiasm, less diligence in looking after themselves, an inability to articulate, and forming a habit of isolation.

It's important that we as adults continue to carry out our responsibilities, especially when others depend on us. Nevertheless, carrying out your responsibilities is one thing, while ensuring that you do it with love and devotion is another thing. It is clear when these aspects are absent, and what touches people's hearts is when someone can do their part in a way that shows they care. When someone is emotionally exhausted, it becomes impossible for them to infuse that kind of compassion and care into their everyday life because they just don't have it in them anymore. They begin to do things out of necessity and without warmth, simply because they are drained of that essential emotional energy. Even in a family dynamic, children and loved ones in the home can end up feeling like the family is just functioning robotically if things are done without that touch of love and affection due to emotional absence. When this happens, we call it being "emotionally unavailable."

So what is emotional availability? I'm sure you have come across people who've complained about a partner, friend, or family member whom they accuse of being emotionally unavailable. Have you ever wondered what exactly people mean when they say that? Being emotionally unavailable refers to a state in which you are not mindful or considerate of how other people feel. Due to your ignorance of other people's emotional states and what they need, those closest to you end up feeling abandoned in the relationship and ultimately dissatisfied because you no longer seem to be willing or capable of meeting their needs. When you are emotionally fatigued, it's easy to become unavailable emotionally to the people around you, and this can strain relationships and cause further harm and emotional stress. Besides being emotionally unavailable to others, someone can be emotionally unavailable to themselves, too. Similar to the previous types of exhaustion we've discussed, this comes about as a result of working so hard and with so narrow a focus that you do not see it coming. You start suppressing how you feel and acting like you are fine when you're not. An example of this is when a single parent is always looking after his or her household and taking care of the children diligently whilst denying their own feelings, which may include loneliness or the desire for a companion. If this sounds like you and you want to have a relationship or to just make friends and form a supportive community around you, it's very important that you don't suppress that need and hide it underneath being busy. Choosing to drown in an endless sea of work every day without nourishing relationships to emotionally support you can lead to burnout and serious emotional exhaustion. It is when you reach this state that you begin falling short of your best, which further degrades your emotional and mental status. You might even start unintentionally treating those around you poorly due to those unaddressed underlying emotions.

The one thing common in those who achieve a happy life and maintain a high level of productivity is thriving emotional health. Unresolved emotions can lead to serious mental health issues such as depression, panic attacks, stress, migraines, and anxiety. Your emotions are like an ecosystem that needs to be balanced and well taken care of. It's also important to let yourself feel your emotions fully, which requires a supportive environment where you feel safe. We are all familiar with the common emotions of happiness, sadness, anger, fear, and anxiety. However, there are many other emotions that are part of being human. By acknowledging and understanding those emotions, you will be able to create space for authentic self-expression, and that promotes emotional rest. Do you ever feel like people just expect you to be happy all the time? We've all felt that pressure at one time or another, especially if you have minors under your watch. Nevertheless, it's important that you make room for yourself to feel any emotion that might spring up within you, process it appropriately, and then move on. Just being able to give yourself permission to grieve, feel sad, happy, or even confused when you need to is a healthy practice. Try to break the pattern of ignoring your emotions and instead be true to how you feel. It's utterly exhausting to pretend to be what you aren't. Maturity means that you finally embrace all of who you are and have learned to emotionally regulate yourself so that you maintain a harmonious ecosystem of emotions. This is the most effective way to stave off emotional exhaustion.

In the next section, let's unpack in detail the various ways you can promote emotional rest to sustainably support emotional health at home, at work, and everywhere in between.

Powerful Tips for Practicing Emotional Rest

Looking after our emotional health is not something that is taught or appreciated in today's society or educational systems. However, with the dramatic increase in awareness of mental health on social media, things are slowly starting to change, and people are becoming more aware of the importance of taking care of their emotional well-being. To help add to your arsenal of strategies for promoting emotional rest in your life, have a look at the following tips to improve your emotional availability for yourself and those around you:

- **Notice and understand your triggers:** Many of the traumatic or destructive experiences we have are imprinted in our subconscious memories, and sometimes certain things that happen in our everyday lives can trigger those embedded wounds buried deep within. A trigger can be anything that reminds you of a traumatic time in your past. An example might be when a stranger speaking to you harshly reminds you of abuse you endured as a child. It then becomes difficult for you to see the person or situation that triggered you from any other perspective because you immediately identify it as a threat or potential source of pain. When this happens between two people in a relationship, trust can be irreparably damaged due to a sufferer's strong emotional triggers getting tied up with a significant other. People respond differently to triggers. Some may experience recurring nightmares while others have constant migraines, and others simply avoid social interactions at all costs. Have you noticed any unhealthy behavioral patterns in yourself that might signify being trapped in an emotional cycle of addiction stemming from a certain trigger? If so, there is always going to be an underlying experience or memory that is causing those behaviors to come out, so it's important to take steps toward addressing them and healing from your trauma. In a growth journal, write down all your triggers that you can identify. It may be necessary to seek out a professional mental health counselor or therapist to help you process the healing that you need, especially if your emotional responses are very strong and/or destructive. It is only when you can finally address your emotional wounds that you will find emotional rest and peace of mind.

- **Avoid your stressors:** Everyone has something that just tips them off. Some of these triggers include bright lights, loud noises, gossip, untidy places, poor communication, tardiness, and the list goes on. Understanding your stressors can help you avoid blindly walking into a situation that may cause emotional distress. Just be mindful of what upsets you. Whenever it's possible to avoid the things that stress you out, try to do so. This is not the same as burying the problem and refusing to address underlying emotions. Of course, there are myriad situations where emotional distress is tied up with loved ones or relationships from which it would be very hard to disentangle yourself. If this sounds like your situation, then consider practicing the "Gray rock method." This is when you show no emotional response to someone who is maliciously trying to get a reaction out of you. This is an effective strategy when dealing with people who have emotionally draining, toxic personalities such as psychopaths, narcissists, and any other sort of manipulative person. With people of this nature, showing any emotion can be a snare for you; even if it's a positive emotion, they can still find a way to use your emotional reaction against you. This is why it's recommended that you be neutral or just emotionless when dealing with them, as this will starve them of the emotional reactions they are trying to encourage. This will buy you some time to get help and devise a way out of the situation.

- **Set strong boundaries to protect your emotional health:** Learning how to set up effective boundaries is a fundamental way to love yourself and look after your emotional well-being.

People can only avoid your triggers if they are informed about what upsets you and what makes you happy. Boundaries mean that you show people what is acceptable behavior and what isn't when it comes to their behavior toward you. This will help those in your life to avoid upsetting you emotionally or violating your trust. Setting boundaries is a skill that can be improved the more you practice doing so with the people around you. For instance, if someone has a habit of always coming in late to work and you end up having to carry their load, that person might not change their behavior unless you tell them upfront how that behavior is affecting you. Many people avoid setting boundaries because they assume it will rock the boat or cause others to dislike them, but the reality is usually just the opposite. People tend to have more respect for people who bravely express what they need and stand up for themselves. So yes, even if it's your kids who are bombarding you with unreasonable demands, good parenting means being able to say no to them and helping them learn how to be supportive and considerate of others. They can only learn these lessons if you communicate clearly what you need from them.

- **Use a worry journal:** Sometimes the mind is filled with so many worries, and if you ask yourself why you are not emotionally okay, it can be hard to decipher the real cause of your mood changes. Keeping a worry journal can help you keep track of the things that bother you, thereby enabling you to address them one by one. A worry journal can also help you see how much you have already overcome, which will encourage you to celebrate your successes and be filled with gratitude. It's easy to fall into a pattern of unfair self-criticism, since we are always expecting more from ourselves. This might not be good for your emotional well-being at all. Learn to accept what you can't change, and actively work on the things you can control. If you are resigned to worrying without taking practical action to resolve emotional issues, you are not making progress. Practice directing your emotional energy toward devising solutions to the problems you are concerned with instead of letting that energy be wasted on ruminating on all the things that might go wrong.

- **Exercise:** Exercise helps your body to release feel-good hormones called endorphins and is an excellent, therapeutic way to maintain your emotional health. Taking a walk, going for a swim, or doing a few stretching exercises in the morning can help alter your emotional state and get you feeling hyped up and energized again. No matter how hectic your work or family demands get, exercise should never be a sidelined activity. All you need is 20 minutes to carry out a meaningful and impactful daily workout session. Lots of people use the excuse that they don't have time to exercise, but that's all in their heads! If you are too busy to go to the gym, you can still get your steps in. For instance, you can go for a walk during lunchtime or use the stairs instead of the elevator. The truth is, where there's a will, there's a way.

- **Walk away from volatile situations:** When a conversation is escalating and about to turn very sour, you can usually see it coming. People tend to say things they don't mean when they are emotionally hurt, and that is why it's important to respectfully walk away from any conversation that looks like it is about to explode into an unpleasant interaction. This is one effective way to protect your emotional well-being, because you prevent yourself from exchanging hurtful words with others that you will regret later. Feuds, disputes, grudges, and any form of relational bitterness cause long-term emotional distress and fatigue. It is draining to be around people who are always tempering their emotions and making you feel unsafe. Therefore, be aware of others' emotional states and give yourself time to cool down if you become upset with someone else. Nothing good can come from exchanging hurtful words when emotions are high.

- **Enlist the help of a mediator to resolve conflict:** Some conflicts and misunderstandings drag on for a long time because the people involved might be in an unhealthy relationship where both parties are communicating poorly. In this case, it's important to ask an intermediary to come in who can play the role of arbitrator. Doing this can help you get to the bottom of the argument and find a swifter resolution to the conflict.

- **Confide in caring and trustworthy friends:** There are people out there who just feel like a safe haven and happy place for others. Try to cultivate great relationships by being proactive in showing others that you care for them and desire a deeper connection. Having people to confide in when you are worried about something helps you maintain your emotional well-being. Loneliness makes people restless, and it's hard to be happy when you don't have deep connections. Make it a priority to set aside time to cultivate meaningful relationships with the people you care about, because they are the ones who will be your pillars of strength when your emotions are tested.

- **Quit any negative self-talk:** Negative self-talk is as crippling as poison is when ingested by a human being. It makes you feel bad about yourself and dysregulates your emotions. If you are chronically facing negative emotions due to your inner critic and unkind thoughts swirling in your mind all day long, take a break and make some time to reprogram your mind and find rest. Sometimes just a change of scenery will help clear your mind and improve your emotional state. When possible, try to find places that inspire you and spend time there instead of in surroundings that promote negative self-talk. You can begin breaking the habit of negative self-talk by interrupting the thoughts as soon as they come up and redirecting them to more positive thoughts.

- **Limit smoking and drinking:** When people are emotionally overwhelmed, many will resort to substance abuse—indulging in smoking, drinking, and taking drugs. All of these can be detrimental not only to your emotional health but also to your physical well-being. Substances are used to escape reality instead of solve problems. But no matter how much you might try to escape reality, the same unresolved problems will be waiting for you. That is why it's better to muster the strength to deal with issues head-on rather than avoiding them. If the process feels overwhelming, try breaking down the task at hand into smaller, manageable daily targets for what you can focus on. By doing what you can each day, you are chipping away at the larger problem and making sustainable progress toward the ultimate solution.

- **Reflect and think about ways to avoid the cycle of unpleasant experiences:** Most of the time, people are contributing to the pain and suffering they are experiencing in their lives in some way. If it's a relationship problem, one of the reasons why you might experience a series of toxic relationships is because you lack self-worth and self-confidence. Thus, attracting toxic partners who tend to take advantage of you might be a constant recurrence in your life. These sorts of unpleasant patterns can make you feel emotionally drained and utterly exhausted, even to the point of just wanting to be numb and avoid relationships altogether. Again, figuring out a solution for breaking this pattern requires reflection and self-awareness, so get professional help or support from your network of friends and family to help you take those first steps.

- **Therapy:** Talking to a licensed professional therapist may help you unearth the unresolved problems that could be causing you emotional burnout. Therapy is also a helpful opportunity to promote personal development and equip yourself with essential life skills that you wouldn't have acquired in conventional educational or corporate institutions. It doesn't have to be an everyday thing. Just seeing a trusted therapist once or twice a month can go a long way in getting the support and help you need to move past emotional trauma. The beauty of quality therapy is that it creates a judgment-free environment for you to fully express your emotions without feeling criticized or threatened in any way. This can ultimately lead to better emotional health and overall well-being.

Your emotional health depends on whether you take action to address your underlying emotional issues. Since emotions aren't tangible things, we tend to take them for granted, and this can eventually lead to bigger problems later on in life, when things finally explode and all those unresolved emotions surface. Now is the best time to start loving yourself by prioritizing your emotional health. Everyone deserves a life free from resentment, anger, and all those unpleasant emotions that only end up draining them. Start your journey today, and do whatever you can to establish a daily emotional check-in and implement the healthy coping skills we've just discussed to achieve true emotional rest.

In the next chapter, we will explore how you can balance the different kinds of rest we have discussed so far with social rest. Let's get right into it!

Chapter 6:

Social Rest

Our social lives encompass how we interact with others and all the interpersonal relationships we have. There are numerous benefits we derive from spending time with loved ones, such as having people to confide in when you are feeling down or in need of advice. You can also enjoy certain hobbies and activities more when you do them with friends or work colleagues. There are plenty of lessons to experience when you connect with others. The bottom line is that your social life is an integral part of your life overall, and it's only when you learn to organize it well that you can get the most benefits out of it whilst avoiding burnout. The flip side of the coin is that our social lives can be extremely difficult to manage, especially when your family grows or when you have to work long hours to sustain your household. Sometimes we end up even getting to a point where we feel like our daily to-do lists are so intense that we don't have time for a social life at all! This is common when someone gets a new job that they aren't used to which demands more time and effort from them than their previous job did. One's social life can easily fall to the wayside when life feels overwhelming, and sadly, this can also lead to loneliness, chronic stress, and even depression. Finding a balance of work and social time is extremely fundamental for ensuring that your lifestyle is meeting both your physiological and social needs.

In this chapter, we will uncover the different strategies you can use to practically eliminate many social stressors and restructure your routine so that your social life can flourish. No matter what age you are, everyone needs genuinely nourishing connections with other people. As human beings, it's in our nature to gravitate toward relationships because that is how we've managed to survive in this world. When someone decides to rely on themselves without room for others to contribute positively to their lives, they shortchange themselves and are put at a disadvantage. There is only so much you can achieve alone, but when you have good relationships with others, you can create a give-and-take situation that offers everyone emotional and physical support when it is needed.

When you have a family, it's even more necessary to have a healthy, supportive network in place, because it takes a village to raise a child. Trying to do everything by yourself can lead to early health problems, fatigue, and dissatisfaction with your life. Thankfully, technology has made it easier to connect with people who might be living similar lifestyles to yours and who are also pursuing the same goals. For instance, if you feel that you barely have time to cook proper meals for your family because of a busy schedule, there are now groups on Facebook or Instagram for mothers and fathers to connect and share ideas for how they can create a healthy work-life balance. Lots of resources are now available in the form of hard copy books, audiobooks, courses, and social clubs that help people learn effective strategies to handle everything that life throws at them.

What's important to note is that any challenge you might face as a parent, and any phase you go through in your life, is something that others before you have experienced. You can learn from others in your community or from older generations in your own family. You don't ever have to feel like you are alone in your situation, as the world has become more connected than ever before. Use the channels at your disposal to reach out and gain new wisdom and insight from those who've learned the lessons you need.

If your social life is doing well, you've probably noticed a positive effect on your health overall. Your physical and mental health will flourish alongside your social life, and when this happens, you'll find you're meeting your goals much easier than before. When a person is struggling with stressful relationships, it's bound to affect their performance in other areas of their life. On the other hand, people who have great social lives tend to excel in their careers and live much happier lives. It may not be obvious on the surface, but social rest is a key aspect of a thriving social life.

Social rest not only entails avoiding people who drain your energy but also developing great relationships that fulfill your social needs. Once you begin honing your relationship-building skills, you'll notice that getting social rest is a natural part of the lifestyle. Not everyone is born with this skill, and sometimes it takes some trial and error to figure out where you are comfortable in terms of a social life. That said, this chapter will give you pointers for ways you can effectively start building great relationships so that your social support system can grow stronger over time.

Let's take a look at some time-tested strategies for building amazing relationships. A well-balanced social life will become part of your armor against long-term stress and burnout.

How to Effectively Build and Maintain Healthy Relationships

Building and maintaining healthy relationships is an integral part of growing up as a healthy and well-adjusted human being. Successful relationships are heavily influenced by the kind of energy you emit and the effort you put forth. All thriving relationships have common characteristics that you typically see from the people involved in them. In the following list, we will unpack the characteristics, values, and principles that can enable you to build long-lasting and successful relationships:

- **Self-advocacy:** Our social relationships can become overwhelming and draining when we fail to express our needs. This tendency to sideline our needs can end up turning us into being highly agreeable people—unable to say no when necessary —and that cycle results in increased burnout. People pleasing is one of the main reasons why social relationships can start to take a toll on someone's life. Learning to be assertive means that you find respectful ways to share your needs and concerns with others instead of keeping things pent up inside and allowing others to walk over you. Self-advocacy entails standing up for yourself whenever you have to and realizing that you have a right to be treated in an appropriate manner. Sometimes parents and children can have unreasonable expectations for each other, and this can be a result of a failure to communicate. To avoid tension and strain in the home, children should help parents understand where they are coming from in a respectful way, and parents must help their children understand their needs as well. By doing this, everyone gets the support they need, but if no one dares to speak up and share sincerely how they feel, then it becomes hard to establish and grow a fulfilling relationship.

- **Self-love:** This is by far the best antidote to solving many relationship problems. When you love yourself, you respect your needs and actively fight for your rights. People who love themselves are less prone to being manipulated and abused by others. However, when you have low self-worth, you might notice that your tolerance level for unacceptable behaviors can be quite high. To grow your self-love and develop a better relationship with yourself, practice self-acceptance. This means that in times when you would typically harshly judge and criticize yourself, choose to show compassion instead. Recognize that the idea that someone has to be "Perfect" is merely a misconception and unrealistic expectation. We all have flaws, and we've all done things we aren't proud of, but that should never be the reason why you treat yourself like you're "less than." The more accepting you are of yourself, the more others will also accept you. This is why solidifying your self-love can inject much healing and growth into your relationships, as people generally tend to reflect how we feel about ourselves.

- **Self-respect and self-esteem:** Respecting yourself and having healthy self-esteem has to do with how you value and perceive yourself. If you recognize and acknowledge your significance and how special you are, you are less likely to allow people to treat you poorly. People should never feel like they can disrespect you or pile an unfair amount of work on you because they think you're a pushover. Self-respect is when you show others how you want them to treat and engage with you. This should happen in every relationship you have, be it with your family, work colleagues, friends, or even strangers. People can only continually violate your values and needs when you allow them to. However, when you are assertive and can set a good example of how to treat others, you can avoid the drama and unpleasant encounters that would socially drain you. Your self-esteem can be cultivated by silencing any limiting beliefs and negative chatter that is going around in your mind. Perhaps as you were growing up, your parents said hurtful things to you that caused you to doubt your worth. It's important that you take time to mindfully sift through those negative narratives and replace them with positive affirmations about who you are and who you want to be. The more negativity you dwell on, the more your self-esteem is bound to hit the rocks. However, when you choose to only focus on the best about yourself and strengthen your good qualities, the bad things which might be making you feel insecure will eventually lose strength and fade away.

- **Self-compassion:** I have a feeling that most of my readers are extremely hard-working. You may be someone who is always giving in your relationships. You work so hard and do so much for others. You push yourself every day and strive for a better life for you and your family. You dare to escape the trap of living a mediocre life. Put simply—you are someone who has so much to be proud of. The people around you get a lot from just having you in their lives. You add so much value to those lives in ways you might not even be conscious of. Somehow, we still find ways to put ourselves down even in the midst of positive reinforcement from friends, coworkers, and family. This cycle of seeing ourselves in negative ways is one of the reasons why we might feel and believe that we don't deserve to have thriving friendships or to be loved. Sadly, when you reinforce this way of thinking, it only manifests in your life, as you push people away and friendships suffer. What causes all of this needless suffering is a lack of self-compassion. We all need great company—

loneliness is not an easy thing. Life is hard without flourishing friendships and close relationships. Allowing yourself to suffer from loneliness and having to carry most of your burdens alone is the direct opposite of self-compassion. When you cultivate compassion for yourself, you start to accept who you are as a complete person and can allow others to help you. Consider taking some time to reflect on your current or failed relationships and consider whether a lack of self-compassion was one of the reasons why those relationships did not succeed.

- **Self-care:** Everyone loves being friends with people who look after themselves. Even children are proud of their parents and will talk about them to their peers if they really seem to have it together. Parents also love it when they see their children taking care of themselves, as it removes a lot of stress and worry. Taking care of yourself means a lot of things, including getting regular health checkups, eating well, getting adequate sleep, doing regular emotional checks, developing healthy coping skills for stressful situations, making time for leisure, setting healthy boundaries, and also standing up for what you believe in. If your relationship with yourself and your life is going well, it becomes easier to then grow healthy social connections.

- **Boundary setting:** When you draw the line and make it clear to others what is acceptable to you and what isn't, that is called setting boundaries. It is an important way of protecting yourself from being used or mistreated by others. People can only treat you badly if you let them. That means, first of all, you have to be clear that you are to be treated with respect when others engage with you. You can also let people know what the consequences are for violating your values, but you've got to stick to them. Setting boundaries is the easy part; what requires more courage and bravery is being assertive and maintaining them in the face of pressure from others. There are lots of examples of setting healthy boundaries, and some them include the following:

determining how much time you will dedicate to social interactions, where you will draw the line when it comes to financial aid you give others, who you will allow into your personal space, and what you won't accept when it comes to how people treat you. If you are a parent, it's important to help your children understand what your role is in their lives, along with their responsibilities when it comes to things like maintaining a tidy household. Respect is shared all around when you can raise a family with expectations and practice for real life, such as letting your children earn a weekly allowance in exchange for doing chores. The only way people can respect your boundaries is if you respectfully let them know and enforce those boundaries. You may need to repeat yourself if this is something people around you aren't used to from you. People can make mistakes and unintentionally cross your boundaries, so try to be patient as those around you learn what is acceptable and what makes you uncomfortable. This way, you're building trust and a relationship from the ground up that is built on mutual cooperation and good communication. It's important to set boundaries within your more intimate relationships as well. Having relationship boundaries in this context includes stating what your sexual needs are and what you will not accept from your significant other. Ultimately, the key to building strong relationships and avoiding relationship stress boils down to communication.

- **Practice being a great communicator:** Being a great communicator involves learning how to express yourself as well as being a great listener. It's hard to get people to do what you need them to or be there for you if you don't communicate your needs clearly. Practice assertive communication and effective body language to send messages to others in a way that is hard to misunderstand or misinterpret. Non-verbal communication includes the things you say with your body, like facial and hand gestures, and these are just as important as the words you say.

People tend to be subconsciously more attentive to your body language and tone more than to the words you are saying, and that is why it's important that you practice being mindful of how you come across to others when you speak. Great communication also has to do with timing. There is always a best time to say something, so if you have an important conversation you'd like to have with someone you care about, check in with them first to see if they're ready to engage with you in the way you need them to. Being a great communicator also involves being honest with people about your energy levels and time constraints. You don't want to promise the world to others only to fall short at the last minute. Everyone has their limits, so learn to say "no" when you need to. It's really okay to be honest about where you stand. By doing so, you create authentic relationships rather than breed resentment because you don't fulfill your promises. That does not provide the positive energy you need to build lasting relationships. Sometimes people avoid saying no because they don't want to disappoint others. However, what's even more hurtful is putting yourself in a position where you deplete and stretch yourself beyond what you are able to bear. It's always best to first consider tending to your own needs before trying to be superwoman or superman to everyone else. I laugh as I write this because I, too, used to be an expert at sidelining my needs while playing superwoman for other people. That only led to many problems, including burnout and fatigue. It can also make you start to resent the very people you are spending so much time and energy to help. Therefore, it's best to be true to yourself and only take on responsibilities when you are sure you can handle them.

- **Have a fun social life:** A vibrant social life is characterized by hobbies and activities that you love doing with positive people. It's so refreshing to have a daily meetup or just somewhere to look forward to where you can connect with others and recharge. It's important to work hard, but don't forget to celebrate and enjoy your life. Companionship goes a long way in bringing that positive, relaxing lifestyle to fruition, especially if everyone in the group is prioritizing those relationships. The only way to form that awesome group of friends is to put yourself out there and socially engage with others. There are many ways to connect with others, so find something that complements your personality and comfort zone. For instance, you don't have to go to parties, clubs, or big social events if those places make you feel super anxious. You can engage with others in a more intimate setting, like a barbecue for a handful of people or a meetup that's focused on a mutual hobby or interest. Without having that downtime to refresh and enjoy connecting with others, our lives can start to feel super draining and rigid. Connecting with others releases the feel-good hormones known as oxytocin and dopamine. By feeling great, our productivity is also positively impacted, and ultimately, you will be less likely to feel drained and overwhelmed with your life.

Restructure your routines in such a way that you are doing things that promote great relationships and eliminate toxicity from your social life. One of the other pivotal parts of people's social lives is social media. On average, people generally spend more than five hours of their time each day on social media. Therefore, if we are relying so much on those platforms to fulfill our social needs, we might as well unpack the ways we can harness them effectively. The next section will show you strategies for how you can use social media wisely without depleting the time set aside for social rest.

How to Use Social Media in a Healthy Way

Everyone has the responsibility to choose how they will utilize social media. It's literally just a tap or click away. We use it on our computers and our phones, and we can access it pretty much any time we want. For many people, social media is also a source of income due to how essential it's become for marketers and influencers alike. When you're using social media not only socially but for work purposes, you're only increasing the risk of burnout. There are two sides to social media: It can be both a blessing and a source of suffering! There are many things we can all learn from the readily available lessons on social media. As long as you're thinking critically about what you're reading, it can be a great place to find educational material and stay up to date with world news. It's also just a fun place to conveniently connect and interact with others around the world. With the development of new features like reels and podcasts, social media has become a great learning source for myriad topics. You can explore the world or just relax with some funny videos. It's a place of great creativity, giving people the chance to share their talents with the world. By taking advantage of all these benefits on social media, you can achieve so much satisfaction in your life while also lowering your stress levels when you use it properly. It's stressful to live a confined life where you always feel like you are living below your potential. However, through social media, you can get a chance to grow and reach greater heights.

Even though social media is a great place to help you build a better life for yourself, it does have a downside that we all have to be mindful of. The disadvantages of using social media can be dire. To help you make sure you don't create burnout and stress in your life, let's unpack the various strategies you can employ:

- **Create social media boundaries:** We all know how social media can be tempting, and before you know it, you have spent hours just mindlessly scrolling while your work is not moving. Social media can influence many people to live sedentary lives and procrastinate on their responsibilities, which ultimately will cause more stress and burnout as you start to work under pressure to try to make up for wasted time. Establish time boundaries whereby you set for yourself a limit on how much time you will spend on social media. Once that time has run out, practice having the discipline to honor it and get on with completing the rest of your daily duties. When it comes to protecting yourself from offensive comments or rude interactions, you can establish space boundaries by making use of your privacy settings. Your accounts are your personal space, and no one has the right to harass you or cause you stress. Block or unfollow people who seem to be troublemakers.

- **Think carefully about who you let follow you:** When it comes to networking, social media is a great place to connect with others and establish meaningful relationships. However, it's important to be careful of who you reach out to or allow to follow you. Being too quick to share your personal information can give people with ill intentions a way to take advantage of you. There are also many scammers and hackers, as well as a great deal of phishing online. When you receive suspicious emails with links to click, avoid clicking on them, as these can be a trap to lead you to some dodgy website where people can steal your private information. When you use it mindfully, social media is a great way to connect with people who share similar interests. It is also a space where you can position yourself to progress in your career and network with other professionals in your field.

- **Encourage real-life connections:** Although it's great and relatively convenient to connect with others on social media, it's still important to meet with your friends and connections in person whenever possible. Virtual "likes" and Zoom are simply never a substitution for genuine, in-person interactions, and it's important to avoid isolating yourself, especially if you're meeting new people online, as there are plenty of people who don't present themselves truthfully. Being present physically with others can also help you avoid living in a fictional world that doesn't represent the reality of life. Some people can get so comfortable with just connecting with others from behind a screen, but that can become very toxic, since we are naturally designed to crave real-life connections. Have the courage to be the one who initiates real-life meetups instead of continuing to settle for online communication. This will help you avoid social media depression or burnout.

- **Avoid making unfair comparisons:** Social media can cause so much emotional and mental stress if you start to use it as a yardstick to measure how well you are doing in life. The things most people portray online are usually heavily edited or just showing the bright side of their lives. Hence, using this to judge yourself causes unnecessary stress. Become your own competition. Strive to be better than your old self instead. That's a far healthier way to better yourself than competing against unrealistic ideals on social media.

Now that we have unpacked the ways you can reinvent your relationships and build a much happier and safer social life, it's time that we uncover how you can also address sensory rest. A lot of sensory stress we incur comes from social media as well. Let's dive into the next chapter to explore more on that topic.

Chapter 7:

Sensory Rest

Everyone has five senses that we use to interact with the world and make sense of things. These include the sense of touch, smell, hearing, taste, and sight. All these senses have specific functions they perform. However, sometimes life becomes too much for your senses, and you get massive information overload from your environment that your brain can't process and manage. "Sensory overload," or "sensory anxiety," occurs when your senses are bombarded with an unbearable amount of input, and this gradually leads to stress and burnout if it is not tempered or stopped. Fortunately, there are many ways to protect your senses and help them function at their best. This chapter will unpack those benefits and also give you practical strategies to help prevent sensory overload and stress.

Sensory overload is a common problem that many people with autism face. In situations where a neurotypical person may have no problem with noise, bright lights, certain food types, or even other people's energies, people with autism might experience a much more intense version of those sensory inputs. It can get so overwhelming for them to be in an environment that triggers their sensory stressors to such a degree, and that is why it's important to show consideration and empathy if there is someone in your life with autism.

Many people with certain personality types are also affected by sensory overload in different ways. You might be someone who doesn't have any problem at all being in loud places or sleeping with your lights on, but for someone else, that environment can be extremely triggering. There are people I know who aren't able to sleep when there is the slightest noise or when lights are on. That environment would make them feel like they are constantly "switched on," thus making it hard for them to get a peaceful rest time. The next time you hear someone complaining about those things, try to see things from their perspective. It's easy to assume that a person is simply needy or a nuisance if you aren't aware of the reality of neurodivergence and varying sensitivities. However, once you understand how sensory overload can cause so much distress in someone, it will be easier for you to exercise compassion and consideration for those who struggle with that issue.

To understand more about sensory overload and whether it's something you actually experience yourself, let's have a look at some of the common symptoms of sensory overload in the next section. Knowing these signs and symptoms will help you to be more accepting of yourself and also avoid situations that may make you feel uncomfortable or cause sensory anxiety.

Common Signs and Symptoms of Sensory Overload

You may have some characteristics that you think are just part of who you are, when in fact, they are an indication of sensory sensitivities. It is essential to be able to manage these effectively to build routines that will protect you from exposure to triggering situations. Let's have a look at some of the common symptoms of sensory overload below:

- **Taste:** Some people are overwhelmed by savory foods or sweets. If you feel like eating certain foods causes you to feel some type of way, it might be an indication of sensory overload resulting from being aversive to certain tastes.

- **Smell:** Some people don't seem bothered when they smell just about anything, with the exception of obviously unpleasant odors. However, you might have come across someone who can't stand being in a room where there is a certain smell coming from food, a strong perfume, or just a pungent body odor. That is an indication of sensitivity to certain smells.

- **Hearing:** Loud noises are not bearable for everyone. People who experience sensory stress related to hearing can have trouble with loud noises, music, or even certain accents. If you ever met someone who could barely stand listening to other people's music or became agitated when exposed to unfamiliar sounds, that was probably an indication that they suffered from a neurodivergent level of hearing sensitivity.

- **Touch:** Touch sensitivities manifest in many different ways, such as feeling restless or uncomfortable when wearing certain fabrics or touching certain textures. Many people don't use bedsheets when they sleep because they feel like they are too cold or the material just makes it hard for them to relax and feel soothed. Another way people experience sensory overload is the simple act of being touched by another person. Physical touch is a love language many people enjoy. However, it's not for everyone. Some people find being touched rather uncomfortable and even stressful. This is why you might hear someone say "I'm not a hugger" or "I don't like touchy people." You might find it hurtful, especially if you are a touchy person yourself. However, you now know that this isn't a personal thing but rather an issue of sensory overload.

- **Sight:** Imagery and many sorts of visual stimulation can lead to sensory overload for some individuals. Have you ever felt like you just needed to rest and be away from phones, television, social media, or anything visually stimulating? That's probably because your sense of sight is giving you signals that it's overwhelmed with the amount of sensory input it's been getting. Spending hours watching videos or just being on social media can cause massive sensory overload, which can make you feel tired and mentally drained.

On the flip side, there are people on the opposite end of the spectrum who actually find comfort in extra sensory stimulation. For instance, babies tend to cry a lot when they aren't touched. They require an overdose of touch to feel comforted and finally get to sleep or just rest. For many adults, the only way they can fall asleep is if they take some time to watch videos before they pass out. Just that act of being exposed to lots of sight stimulation helps them to fall asleep. This is unusual, since typically, screen time can affect the production of melatonin.

Understanding your sensory triggers can help you understand how to manage them so they don't end up affecting your relationships or hindering your access to quality rest in all its forms.

How to Find Rest From Sensory Overload and Stress

Below are ways that you can overcome any form of sensory overload and create a more soothing lifestyle for yourself:

- **Communicate with others about what causes you sensory stress:** When someone has sensory triggers, it can put others off, as they might be labeled as being demanding or overly sensitive. Respectfully express your needs to help others understand your struggles. This way, they will be more empathetic toward you. Also, accept who you are and avoid giving in to the pressure of being like everyone else. You are special and unique just as you are, and having these sensory triggers doesn't make you a bad person. You deserve the support and respect from those who call themselves your friends or loved ones. Help people support you by being proactive and informing them about your situation.

- **Create an environment that is supportive of your sensory needs:** Since your workplace and your room are probably the places you are most likely to spend most of your time, it's important that you take action and talk to people who can help accommodate your sensory needs. For instance, if you are someone who is affected by loud noises and has severe anxiety around other people, then it would be best to move into a job that is not in a busy office. For example, if you can manage to get a remote job that allows you to work from home, this can help you to get the sensory rest you need from social interactions. If bright lights make you feel uncomfortable, you can choose to make your room cozy and dim by using dim lights or a lamp instead of big, bright lights that cause you discomfort. You could also use fleece for your blankets and bedding instead of using sheets or uncomfortably textured material if you are sensitive to touch. Also, be sure to take some time alone for yourself so you can recharge and clear your mind. There are so many options to choose from, including: taking a walk, having a massage, showering and then resting in a sauna, trying out aromatherapy, using noise-canceling headphones, taking an ice bath or using bath salts, doing regular breathing exercises, journaling, meditating, practicing yoga, doing stretching exercises, and keeping a cozy, warm home that is well heated. Being with loved ones who make you feel happy also helps to calm your nerves and keep you in a great mood.

When people experience sensory overload, their mind tells them that they are in some form of threatening situation. This makes your body react with the flight, fight, or flee response, and your whole system is thrown into survival mode. Being in survival mode keeps you from feeling rested. If someone continues to live in survival mode all the time, that's when things like mental breakdown, stress, and burnout become imminent. To avoid this, it's important to create and maintain an environment that is conducive to your sensory needs.

In the following chapter, we will unpack various ways you can incorporate the next form of rest you need—spiritual rest.

Chapter 8:

Spiritual Rest

We spend so much of our time tending to our physical needs, from the time we wake up until the time we lay our heads on the pillow. Our concern for our physical well-being is prioritized, and that allows us to live comfortable and healthy lives. But just as the flesh flourishes and glows when it's well looked after through good nutrition, exercise, and rest, our spirits need rest and attention, too, in order to thrive and sustain us. Your spirit is your inner being—it's essentially the real *you*. Your body is the house in which your spirit lives. We need to keep our houses in good condition, but their importance can never be compared with how important *you* are. When there is a robbery or a house is set on fire, people's concerns are for the people inside the house. Physically, it wouldn't make sense to value your house more than you value yourself. Similarly, it's important that we place value on the spirit and invest our time and resources into keeping it in good condition.

The quality of your life is heavily dependent on the condition of your spirit. If your inner being isn't doing well, your life will also start to reflect that underlying problem. Think of it this way: Imagine your spirit is a tree, and then all the different aspects of your life are the fruits of that tree. If a fruit is unhealthy, it doesn't make sense to just apply medication or treatment to it. Instead, you have to check the roots of the tree to see if the tree is getting enough sunlight, nutrients, and water. If the tree is healthy, all the fruits of that tree will also be healthy. That means, when your spirit is doing well, every other aspect of your life will follow suit. Those aspects of your life can be things such as your social life, health, career, spiritual life, and emotional well-being. If you feel like your life is falling apart and things just keep spiraling out of control, a good place to start diagnosing the problem is checking in with how your spirit is doing.

Your spirit, soul, and heart are where all the decisions you make come from. Looking after those components of who you are gives you the strength and wisdom to make good decisions and take healthy risks that can unleash your full potential.

Now, I would like you to reflect on how you spend your time each day. How much of that time would you say you devote to nurturing your spirit, ensuring that you unburden yourself from all the things that might be wearing down your heart? We rarely ever miss out on our physical meals, and if we do miss out even once on a meal, we might end up getting agitated and super angry, barely able to focus on anything. However, when it comes to our spirits, most people go days without intentionally looking after their spiritual needs. Let's revert back to the tree example to help you understand how our spirits work in similar ways. If you don't water a tree for a few days, that tree might still look the same and seem like everything is fine. However, that's just an illusion because inside, the tree will be slowly dying. It's only a matter of time before you start to see visible signs of wilting and drying until the tree completely dies. This, too, is what happens when you become busy and allow yourself to be occupied with everything except looking after your spirit. You might seem like you are okay and pretty much the same old you. However, as time goes on, your life will start to show signs of regression or stagnation because the aspect that's responsible for driving you toward achieving your dreams is not being looked after. This is when problems such as mental health issues, failed relationships, missed opportunities, and failed goals start to pop up, and you will begin to notice that something is not right. Damage control costs a lot more than preventing problems from sprouting in the first place. Investing in your spiritual rest is one sure way to protect your life from the problems you can avoid.

Creating a lifestyle whereby your spirit is always nourished and immersed in positive energy thoughts will help you to let go of many problems that make you feel stressed and burned out. Using positive words of affirmation can help to crystalize positive changes. As human beings, we have an innate need to feel loved and connected with others in harmonious ways. Trying to ignore those spiritual needs makes us fed up with the same old routines of just working and focusing on our physiological needs. Our ability to perform well physically and mentally is highly dependent on how well we look after our inner beings.

Another common dilemma that makes us feel restless in our lives is when we don't have the answers to important existential questions. These are questions like, "Who am I?" "What's my purpose?" and "How can I live the life I was created for?" No matter how much success we might achieve on the outside, we can miss out on what we were truly created for if our spirits and souls do not find true rest. True fulfillment and rest for our souls are only found when we take the time to discover those answers. You can do this by exploring different areas of interest until you find what makes your heart dance. Without knowing your purpose and what makes you happy, you may experience a lot of unhappiness and emptiness. Sometimes your life might even make you feel like you are no different from a leaf being blown in any direction the wind blows. When you live without answering the question of what fulfills you and brings you peace and meaning, eventually, you may end up losing enthusiasm for life in general. All this goes to show us that indeed, our happiness lies in allowing ourselves to discover what we are good at and then making the most of it. It lies in being in touch with our inner selves and allowing ourselves to heal from any wounds that might have been inflicted on us in the past.

To help you learn ways you can promote spiritual rest, let's have a look at the next section, which will give us tips on sustainable spiritual practices to foster spiritual rest.

Tips for Finding Spiritual Rest

Finding spiritual rest entails having a maintenance plan in place for the well-being of your spirit. This means that each and every day, your spirit has to be looked after in one way or another. The more you can diligently take care of your spirit, the less stress and burdens you will have to endure. Just as our bodies rarely get sick when we are looking after them, our spirits can remain vibrant when we take care of them, too. Taking care of your spirit is the fundamental way to truly love yourself. As you continue to do so, you will start to realize that you have more to give to others because of the abundance of your spirit. However, when our spirits aren't healthy, there is no doubt that looking after others ceases to be a joyful experience rather becomes burdensome and draining. To help you with ideas for things you can do to look after your spirit well, take a look at the following tips:

- **Start or finish your day with positive daily affirmations or mantras:** It's become so easy for us to just automatically look at our phones the moment we open our eyes every morning to check our social media accounts and messages. Our phone is usually also the last item we focus on just before we sleep, sometimes forgetting our bedtime prayers. I say this because I, too, used to get carried away like that until I realized how spiritually and mentally unhealthy it was for me to continue indulging in those habits. Positive daily mantras and affirmations can breathe life into your days. They give us a sense of direction on how we ought to be and where we need to go. They help us to be intentional about how we live our lives. When we starve ourselves of such spiritual practices, we become vulnerable to other people's influence. You can also start to be affected by what's happening in your life until you feel like you are losing control of it completely. By choosing positive affirmations, you give yourself a sense of purpose and start to live with intention rather than being a victim of circumstances.

- **Participate in volunteer work:** Philanthropy is a beautiful way to positively contribute to the improvement of other people's lives. Volunteering through any means possible, even if it's just offering your time, manpower, or donations for material things, can help to give you a sense of fulfillment and purpose that you rarely find when you are only self-serving.

- **Invest in reading spiritual books:** Read good spiritual books that can help you to learn different ways to elevate your spirit. Attending a study group with others can give you a chance to learn what sort of spiritual practices work best for others. Setting aside a fraction of your time each day to read new things gives you a chance to grow spiritually. Just as you can improve how you take care of yourself physically, new knowledge and great spiritual habits can help you grow in the way you look after your spirit.

- **Journal about your spiritual growth:** A spiritual journal is an excellent way to remind yourself of how many challenges you have already overcome so far. Sometimes when we achieve something, we immediately start wanting something more and become downcast, forgetting to be grateful for what we already have. In a spiritual journal, you can keep an account of all the things you have already overcome, and reading this can help you to maintain faith and confidence in your ability to overcome the rest of your challenges. A spiritual journal can also help you to focus on things that matter and keep you dedicated and focused on achieving your goals.

- **Watch spiritual movies:** Many movies have a beautiful way of suggesting different ways to invigorate our spirits. Taking time to watch those movies is both fun and inspirational. It can awaken your spirit and shake you out of any spiritual slumber you might be experiencing. Search for movies that can help you overcome the challenges you might be going through and write them down in your spiritual journal. YouTube is also a great resource to connect to other spiritual people and be a part of a growing community. By subscribing to your favorite channels, you can receive a constant supply of new ideas for ways to bring out the best in your spiritual life.

- **Participate in spiritual hobbies:** Your spiritual journey requires creativity and innovativeness to make it fun and memorable. Participating in activities like singing, dancing, mantra reciting challenges, and other spiritual clubs or competitions can help you to feel more refreshed and encouraged in your spiritual walk.

- **Search for worship music you enjoy:** Don't we all love music and the mesmerizing impact it has on us? Perhaps you might be tired of hearing the same songs over and over again. You can create your own playlist and regularly update it as you discover new songs that stir your heart. When you feel down, it's always a great practice to elevate your spirit through music. Music helps us dream and imagine all sorts of possibilities. Take some time to find the kind of music that makes your heart dance with joy.

- **Build a strong friendship circle with your spiritual brothers and sisters:** When we are united as one with our brothers and sisters of similar spiritual beliefs, we become powerful and complete. We are like a body, and everyone has a part to play. By connecting with others and building strong relationships, we establish a supportive structure that enables us to withstand the storms of life. There is nothing so difficult as feeling alone in life. You can take the initiative to help unite people by either inviting friends to your house for lunch or having an outdoor picnic. Doing these activities can help people avoid needlessly suffering alone or feeling like a stranger among our own spiritual brothers and sisters. The more love you spread, the more love you will receive in turn. Easy peasy, right? I'm sure you can do it!

- **Overcome and let go of any guilt by confessing your wrongdoings:** All of us err; no one is perfect. Learning to have self-compassion and letting go of the things we did in the past helps us to move forward positively. Negative reflection is when you keep pondering on your faults and using them to put yourself down. If you feel like you are trapped in this cycle, please consider taking some time to empty your heart. Going through that process allows you to deal with the elephant in the room and not continue to let your past haunt you. Forgive yourself and others, as this will give you rest and freedom from resentment, anger, shame, guilt, and all sorts of unpleasant emotions which can vex your spirit.

- **Create a positive atmosphere in your spiritual place of worship:** The atmosphere we are in influences us to either want to continue to show up at certain places or not. For some people, when they feel like there are "bad vibes" or "negative energy" in their places of worship, they resort to complaining or give up on going there again. However, this ought not to be the case for spiritually mature people. Your intuition can give you the eyes to notice that something is wrong when you visit certain places. It's better to choose to be the change rather than just expose the negativity of that environment. Have the courage to suggest ideas on how to improve things, but most importantly, let your presence and how you treat others be what inspires everyone else to change. Such is the path of a truly mature spiritual person— always bringing light and life wherever you go. Help people find spiritual rest by taking an interest in them, praying for them, or just offering a listening ear. Also, give yourself permission to confide in others when you are spiritually burdened and allow them to support you as well.

As you commit to a life of loving yourself through looking after your spirit and nourishing it with positivity, many of the desires of your heart will be fulfilled. Let your anchor and greatest support structure be your investment in how you look after your spirit. It's hard for the winds of life to break a spiritually strong and tenacious person.

In the last chapter, we will uncover the last form of rest—creative rest. Let's explore how you can be rested in a holistic way and regain the lifestyle of your dreams.

Chapter 9:

Creative Rest

Are there ever times when you feel like you have just been going through the motions and are simply out of touch with your creative side? Do you ever feel like your life follows a rigid routine that you are now tired of? Maybe initially, you loved your job, but since there hasn't been room for you to grow and evolve into better positions or roles, everything just feels like you are being held hostage at a job where you barely ever feel alive. This can happen in relationships, too. If there isn't growth, it becomes difficult to feel satisfied or happy in those relationships. It takes creativity to experience progression and change in our lives. We have all faced those circumstances where you just feel so stifled and constantly find yourself daydreaming of another life that allows you to express who you are and what you are good at without restraints. The great news is that no matter how dire your situation may seem when it comes to creative rest, it's certainly a goal you can achieve, because all you need is *creativity*.

Finding creative rest has to do with allowing yourself to think outside the box, try new things, escape the ordinary, and dare to embrace change, not only here and there but as often as possible. It's in finding ways to make your day-to-day responsibilities not feel boring or mundane.

Realize that your life can only be as fun and cool as you allow it to be. If you settle for doing things without having fun or play too small even when you know you have all it takes to do better, that is another sign of stifled creativity. When we don't enjoy what we have to do often, this leads to creative fatigue. This is when you just feel boxed in and aren't able to take pleasure in your life.

People who are good at making ordinary things feel special and who choose to find joy in simple things are usually very creative. No matter what age you are or what role you have in your family, it's never too late to create a life that is filled with adventure, thrilling changes, and beauty.

No matter how busy your schedule might be, it's never too late to choose to pause and take in the beauty around you. Life doesn't have to feel mechanical. You aren't a robot, so please make a commitment to never treat yourself as such. You deserve to enjoy yourself, explore the world, and go after the dreams of your heart courageously. The only way creativity can flourish is if you are willing to escape your comfort zone and try new things. You also need to make room for failure and choose to see it as part of your learning journey. People who don't try anything new don't get to experience how talented they are. They remain stuck in the same way of life, which is really sad. To ensure that this doesn't become your fate, let's unpack the various ways you can empower yourself so that your creativity can start expressing itself in every area of your life.

Tips for Attaining Creative Rest

Unleashing your creative side requires you to have a growth mindset. You have to accept that at first, things might not go well or may even feel awkward. However, the more you hone your creative skills, the better you will become at doing anything you set your mind to. Below are some ideas for how you can stir up and free your creativity:

- **Try out new things regularly:** You will be astounded by how many things you enjoy if you dare to try. Of course, the fear of the unknown or of failure can get in the way, but it can only hold you back if you choose to let it. It's important to get over your fear of failing and just try. This is how you get to find yourself and discover strengths you would have never known you had. Invite a friend over and try out new things together; it's fun when you grow together and build bonds. For example, you can test out and work on improving your culinary skills, learn a new language, birdwatch, learn interior designing lessons, try out new workout routines, sew new clothes, play puzzle games, make a creative sculpture, create a memes collection to improve your sense of humor, and sing away your worries. As you can see, there are many things waiting for you to explore, just have faith and challenge yourself to try at least one new thing each day.

- **Watch television and listen to music:** More than just providing us with entertainment, television and music is a world in which we all can find inspiration. You can improve your eloquence and sharpen your intelligence when you are exposed to the creative wonder of movies and many other programs available on mainstream media. The media also helps you to see how others push themselves and live better lives by chasing their dreams despite fierce competition or challenges. This in turn will help you to have more faith in yourself. Movies and soothing music can help you feel well-rested, as they uplift your soul.

- **Spend quality time with loved ones:** Out of the beautiful things life has to offer, being with our loved ones is one of the best. People we love and care about have a way of encouraging us to step up and go after our dreams. They can also help you discover your strengths and make you mindful of the weaknesses you have that may be keeping your life stagnant. By spending time with family and friends, you get a chance to gain perspective and unlock the hidden potential in you. Always choose to spend your time with people who inspire you.

- **Dance to the beat of your heart and soul:** In a world where the pressure to fit in and be accepted by others seems rampant, it can be inevitable that you lose touch with what truly matters to you in a bid to please others. We are designed to thrive and excel in areas where we are naturally gifted. If you follow your heart's most beautiful dreams and desires, you are bound to harness your gifts and succeed in doing so. It's easy to be creative in areas where you are born to excel in, and that is why it's important that you get in touch with your soul's deepest longings and honor them. Also, remember to let go of the pressure to always create and learn to celebrate who you are and where you are now.

- **Travel:** The ways people live their lives around the world are diverse. Traveling helps you to gain a broader perspective on many things in life as you learn about different cultures. For instance, if you travel overseas, you will be exposed to new cuisines. You might end up adopting new methods for cooking your own meals at home. Other countries are well known for having great etiquette and manners; for instance, in Japan, people bow when they greet you. This and more can help you learn about diverse values and practices.

- **Personal grooming:** As you age, your looks will evolve along with your personal style. Taking time to look after yourself and maintain a clean look, trying out various clothing options, and learning to improve your social etiquette can help you to become someone who not only looks good on the outside but has excellent character from within. To take it a step further, consider working with a life coach or taking online courses to bring you closer to the vision you have for yourself, both personally and professionally.

- **Advocate for change where you live:** Our minds love familiarity; that is why we face so much struggle whenever we try to do something new that takes us outside our comfort zones. Become the person who encourages people around you to try out new things, go to new places, and do things differently. For instance, you can choose to rearrange your furniture at home or continuously upgrade your decorations. Making sure that your home has a beautiful interior helps to create an atmosphere that inspires you to work or continue to better yourself.

- **Take creative classes:** If you feel like finding creative rest is rather difficult for you, it may be worthwhile to consider taking creative classes in any field you might find enjoyable. Being in an environment that grooms and nurtures your creativity helps you to find many other ideas for creative rest you can include in your lifestyle. Creative classes you can take include cooking classes, music lessons, art classes, self-defense and martial arts, or computer programming. All these sorts of classes promote creative thinking, which you will in turn use to reel in more creative rest ideas for your daily routine.

- **Add adventures to your calendar:** When we think of our calendars, we usually imagine all sorts of work and assignments that are waiting for us to attend to. Your calendar doesn't always have to be this way; you can make it more exciting to look at by adding things you look forward to doing. Just having a quick glance at those things gives you more energy to get the tiresome tasks out of the way as quickly as possible so you can finally get to do those exciting activities on your calendar.

- **Take time to appreciate art:** Visiting museums and galleries is a creative way to find inspiration. If you cannot do so physically, there is always the option of doing virtual tours. Even YouTube now has lots of content made available free of charge for touring many museums and galleries that are located in almost every part of the world. Who says having a plane ticket is the only way to know what's going on the other side of the world? Doing your virtual tours can also teach you about new places and inspire travel ideas for the future.

- **Daydream:** We sometimes see the habit of daydreaming as being rather silly, but in essence, most dreams are conceived during that time. Take a few minutes in the morning or in the evening just before bed to daydream about the kind of future you wish to create for yourself. Imagine where you'd like to be in a few years after you've achieved a professional goal. Fill in the details to make the vision as clear as possible. Painting a visual picture like this will help you find direction and a path to happiness and personal satisfaction. Daydreaming can certainly take us to places where our souls can find a lot of inspiration.

There is so much that you can contribute to your life and the lives of those around you if you dare to trust and believe in yourself. Life requires us to dare to explore and rise up to the occasion. If you feel stuck and unsure of how you can do so, consider taking a walk in nature and use that time to meditate on the things you wish you could do. Ask yourself what's stopping you from getting there and what it will take for you to cross over the chasm of your current life to your new life of boundless creativity. For every problem, there is always a solution waiting to be discovered. For everything you don't ask about or try, the answer is always no. Each day provides you with another chance to try things again intelligently and creatively. My question is, will you finally do so from now on? I believe you will. It is only the limitations we place on ourselves that have the power to hold us back. Thankfully, the power to free ourselves from those limitations is also within ourselves. The time has come for you to no longer just survive the days of your life. It's time to soar and live to the fullest!

Conclusion

Our modern world will continue to throw challenges at us throughout our lives, but when we are prepared with the tools for self-care and rest, we can meet them head-on without risking burnout. By ensuring that your life has all the seven kinds of rest included in your daily routines—including physical, mental, emotional, social, sensory, spiritual, and creative rest—you can set a foundation of joy and sustainable productivity. Sounds easier said than done? Perhaps. However, you have the willpower and grit to fight for the life you want. The fact that you took the time to read this book already proves how determined you are. I have no doubt that you will be able to use that determination to be intentional about creating the quality of life you've always wished for. Now that you've read this book, there's no excuse to keep procrastinating any longer. Your well-being deserves better than the back burner.

Stress and burnout are just your body and mind pleading to you that something has to change. Modern life is filled with demands and busy schedules that constantly steer us away from introspection and self-care. Male or female, and whatever age you are now, nothing has the power to keep you tied to a lifestyle you no longer want except yourself. I believe that this day marks the time when things will begin to turn around for you. You can now take the reins and move your life in a more healthy direction for every aspect of your body and mind. You've worked so hard to create the life you have been living up until now, so now it's time to reward yourself with the bliss and rest you deserve. Your future self will thank you for the effort you're putting in now, as will your friends, family, loved ones, and everyone else in your orbit. Become the powerful advocate of change you are destined to be. Most importantly, never forget to trust and have faith in yourself—you've got this!

About the Author

Allison Hay lives outside of Seattle with her two teenage daughters. She spent more than 20 years working in corporate Human Resources departments and burning the candle at both ends trying to keep up with her work, family, and modern life. She has always enjoyed writing, but this started to really take off during the pandemic. Through this book, she aspires to help adults who are struggling to balance their lives find a way to incorporate rest and put an end to chronic stress. Burnout is very real. However, so is the answer for ending it. This book is here to help you discover those answers for yourself.

If this book has inspired you to take the leap and forge a new life free of burnout and chronic stress, please spread the word and leave a review so others can find the same guidance.

References

Bamae, Body, Mind, Earth. (2021, October 27). *100 Creative Ways to Take a Break*. Bamae. https://www.bamae.com/blogs/mindful-thoughts/100-creative-ways-to-take-a-break

Brodie, J. (2023, March 26). *6 Ways to Embrace Rest as a Spiritual Discipline - Explore the Bible*. Biblestudytools.com. https://www.biblestudytools.com/bible-study/explore-the-bible/6-ways-to-embrace-rest-as-a-spiritual-discipline.html

Cafasso, J. (2019, April 9). *What Is Emotional Exhaustion and How Do You Fix It?* Healthline. https://www.healthline.com/health/emotional-exhaustion

Eatough, E. (2021, June 1). *22 ways to treat and navigate emotional exhaustion | BetterUp*. Www.betterup.com. https://www.betterup.com/blog/emotional-exhaustion

Hailey, L. (2022, April 15). *How to Set Boundaries: 5 Ways to Draw the Line Politely*. Science of People. https://www.scienceofpeople.com/how-to-set-boundaries/

McDaniel, J. (2019, December 16). *How to Rest Your Mind: 6 Tips*. Psych Central. https://psychcentral.com/blog/six-simple-ways-to-rest-the-mind#1

Santos-Longhurst, A. (2018, October 26). *How to Treat and Prevent Mental Exhaustion*. Healthline; Healthline Media. https://www.healthline.com/health/mental-exhaustion

Skipping Stones. (2020a, January 9). *Are You In Need Of Spiritual Rest?* Skipping Stones. https://www.goskippingstones.com/blog/rest5

Skipping Stones. (2020b, March 13). *Finding Creative Rest*. Skipping Stones. https://www.goskippingstones.com/blog/2020/3/3/part-7-finding-creative-rest

Skipping Stones. (2020c, March 15). *Finding Sensory Rest*. Skipping Stones. https://www.goskippingstones.com/blog/sensory-rest

Skipping stones. (2019, November 25). *Physical Rest - What is it and how to Get It*. Skipping Stones. https://www.goskippingstones.com/blog/2019/11/22/rest-part2

Summa Health. (2020, February 17). *7 Health Benefits to Getting a Good Night's Rest*. Www.summahealth.org. https://www.summahealth.org/flourish/entries/2020/02/7-health-benefits-to-getting-a-good-nights-rest

Sweekly. (2017, October 16). *8 ways to take a creative break*. Medium. https://artplusmarketing.com/8-ways-to-take-a-creative-break-566d531fcf7

Tartakovsky, M. (2018, April 29). *7 Reasons You Might Resist Rest and How to Get Mental Rest*. Psych Central. https://psychcentral.com/blog/how-to-really-rest#tips-to-rest

Team Zoella. (2020, August 31). *8 Ways to Create Healthy Boundaries Online*. Zoella. https://zoella.co.uk/2020/08/31/8-ways-to-create-healthy-boundaries-online/

White, H. (2022, December 21). *7 Types of Rest: The Key to Becoming the Prepared Adult*. Amshq.org. https://amshq.org/Blog/2022-12-21-7-Types-of-Rest